teach®

recruitment

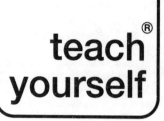

recruitment
edward peppitt

CORPORATION OF LONDON LIBRARIES	
CLO929857	
Cypher	07.02.04
658.311PEP	£9.99
RB	

For over sixty years, more than 40 million people have learnt over 750 subjects the **teach yourself** way, with impressive results.

be where you want to be
with **teach yourself**

For UK order enquiries: please contact Bookpoint Ltd, 130 Milton Park, Abingdon, Oxon OX14 4SB. Telephone: +44 (0)1235 827720. Fax +44 (0)1235 400454. Lines are open 09.00–18.00, Monday to Saturday, with a 24-hour message answering service. Details about our titles and how to order are available at www.teachyourself.co.uk

For USA order enquiries: please contact McGraw-Hill Customer Services, PO Box 545, Blacklick, OH 43004-0545, USA. Telephone: 1-800-722-4726. Fax: 1-614-755-5645.

For Canada order enquiries: please contact McGraw-Hill Ryerson Ltd, 300 Water St, Whitby, Ontario L1N 9B6, Canada. Telephone: 905 430 5000. Fax: 905 430 5020.

Long renowned as the authoritative source for self-guided learning – with more than 30 million copies sold worldwide – the *Teach Yourself* series includes over 300 titles in the fields of languages, crafts, hobbies, business, computing and education.

British Library Cataloguing in Publication Data: a catalogue record for this title is available from the British Library.

Library of Congress Catalog Card Number: on file.

First published in the UK 2003 by Hodder Headline Ltd, 338 Euston Road, London, NW1 3BH.

First published in US 2003 by Contemporary Books, a Division of the McGraw-Hill Companies, 1 Prudential Plaza, 130 East Randolph Street, Chicago, IL 60601 USA.

This edition published 2003 ✓ 0340799897

The 'Teach Yourself' name is a registered trade mark of Hodder & Stoughton Ltd.

Copyright © 2003 Edward Peppitt

In UK: All rights reserved. No part of this publication may be reproduced or transmitted in any form or by any means, electronic or mechanical, including photocopy, recording, or any information storage and retrieval system, without permission in writing from the publisher or under licence from the Copyright Licensing Agency Limited. Further details of such licences (for reprographic reproduction) may be obtained from the Copyright Licensing Agency Limited, of 90 Tottenham Court Road, London W1T 4LP.

In US: All rights reserved. Except as permitted under the United States Copyright Act of 1976, no part of this publication may be reproduced or distributed in any form or by any means, or stored in a database or retrieval system, without the prior written permission of Contemporary Books.

Typeset by Servis Filmsetting Ltd, Manchester

Printed in Great Britain for Hodder & Stoughton Educational, a division of Hodder Headline Ltd, 338 Euston Road, London NW1 3BH, by Cox & Wyman Ltd, Reading, Berkshire.

Papers used in this book are natural, renewable and recyclable products. They are made from wood grown in sustainable forests. The logging and manufacturing processes conform to the environmental regulations of the country of origin.

Impression number   10 9 8 7 6 5 4 3 2 1

Year   2009 2008 2007 2006 2005 2004

Permission to use the artwork from *People Managers* on pages 68–9 is gratefully acknowledged.

contents

introduction

This book is ideal for anyone who needs to recruit a new member of staff. Whether you currently work alone, or for a multi-national organization, you will find the practical, step-by-step approach invaluable.

The book covers the complete recruitment process, from recognizing that you need to recruit to introducing your appointed candidate into your organization effectively. Each stage is fully explained:

- looking at alternatives
- planning
- outlining the role and the ideal candidate
- recruiting internally
- using agencies
- using the internet
- advertising
- shortlisting
- interviewing
- testing
- selecting
- appointing
- running induction programmes.

With sample forms, and examples of the paperwork and processes described, this book will equip you with every skill you need to identify and appoint the right new staff member for your organization.

part

one
deciding to recruit

01

why are you recruiting?

In this chapter you will learn:

- whether or not you need to recruit
- how to predict the need to recruit.

Perhaps a member of your staff has resigned. Or maybe your organization is growing at such a rate that you need to take on more people. Whatever your need to recruit, it is essential that you look at all the alternatives before you start. With careful planning, you may find that you don't need to recruit after all.

Do you need to recruit?

If you are planning to recruit a team member to a new role in your organization then you have probably given the matter considerable thought already. You should know the answers to the following questions:

- Why is the new position necessary?
- What are the roles and responsibilities of the new position?
- Who will the position report to?
- How senior is the position?
- What skills and experience would be required to perform the role?
- Could the role be covered by any other position within the organization?

If, however, you are recruiting because an existing member of staff has retired or resigned, you should think carefully about whether you need to replace them or not. Consider the following questions:

- Why has the existing job holder resigned?
- How has the role developed over time?
- Will the role continue to exist for the foreseeable future?
- Could any other job holder handle the additional responsibility of part/all of the role?
- How important is the role? Is the role central to the organization?
- How does the role contribute to the overall objectives of the department, and ultimately of the organization?

The answers to some of these questions should confirm whether or not you actually need to recruit. Many people in business consider that a resignation is a good opportunity to look again at their staffing requirements. Here are two practical examples:

Case 1

A direct marketing agency employed a part-time PA for one of the company directors. They also employed someone part-time in their sales team, whose role was to turn the salespeople's notes into well-presented proposals. The part-time PA resigned because she was getting married and moving to London. The agency recruited a replacement PA, also on a part-time basis. In fact, the part-time sales team member was looking for a full-time position. He would have been interested in a role that encompassed both generating the proposals and working as a PA. If the agency had regarded their PA's resignation as an opportunity, they may have thought of this possibility themselves. Instead, the part-time sales team member also resigned shortly afterwards to move to a full-time position elsewhere.

Case 2

A high street retailer of maps and travel books employed someone on the shop floor who was soon to retire. Before he left, the managers got together to consider his replacement. After a lengthy discussion, they concluded that the demand for paper maps was such that a full-time retail staff member could no longer be justified. However, the demand for digital maps was soaring, and staff in that department were fully stretched. So it was agreed that John's retirement was a good opportunity to strengthen the digital maps department, and reduce the paper maps department by one.

These two examples show how important it is to use a resignation or retirement as an opportunity to look carefully at your current staffing needs. Perhaps you do not need to recruit after all?

What are the alternatives?

Vacancies tend to arise for two reasons. Either your organization has grown or developed, or one of your existing staff is leaving. In either case, it is worth considering the alternatives before starting the recruitment process:

Reorganization

Can the functions and responsibilities of the role be redefined? Or reassigned? In either case, you may not have to recruit a new staff member. Perhaps someone working for you is always asking for more responsibility? If so, could they handle some or all of the responsibility of the outgoing job holder's role in addition to their own? Perhaps the role need not be performed by someone so senior? Maybe the role needs someone more senior still? A reorganization of the team or role can often mean that you will either not have to recruit after all, or that you need to recruit someone with different skills and experience to the outgoing job holder.

Outsourcing

Could the role be outsourced, either to freelance staff or to a third party organization? A vacancy provides a good opportunity to consider this option. If the role is not central to the business, the argument for outsourcing can be compelling.

Automation

Can the role be automated, either now or in the foreseeable future? If so, there is a strong case for assessing the viability of automation, rather than employing a new staff member to the role.

Type of role

If the role is currently performed by someone full-time, could it be performed part-time? Would this allow greater flexibility for the role? Would this saving then allow you to strengthen a different part of the team or department?

Assessing the alternatives to recruitment is vital, and is a step that should be taken every time a vacancy arises.

Predicting the need to recruit

If a member of your staff leaves unexpectedly, then of course you will argue that you could not have predicted it. After all, they seemed happy in their job, and the reasons they gave for leaving appeared genuine, and unrelated to the organization.

In many cases, this is so. However, organizations are increasingly looking at their staffing needs of the future, and summarizing these as part of a constantly developing business plan. This prediction of staffing requirements is often referred to as 'workforce planning'. The principle of workforce planning is as follows:

Step 1: Estimating workforce requirements

The business plan states the organization's objectives for the coming period (usually one year). It also lays down specific targets in terms of sales and costs. Your role is to estimate both the number of staff and the skills that you require in order to meet the targets laid out in the business plan.

- Will more or fewer staff be required in each department/team?
- Do you have any specific skills shortages?
- Will changes to working patterns be required?
- Will any services need to be centralized or outsourced?

Step 2: Audit your current staff

You have established what you need from your workforce to deliver the objectives and targets in the business plan. Now you need to audit what you already have. Where in your organization do you have staff wastage? Where are you most understaffed? What skills do your staff already possess? Where are you short?

Step 3: Summarize the skills and staff gap

If you know what skills and staff you need, as well as what you have already got, you should be able to summarize the shortfall (as well as when specifically the shortfall is likely to occur). From this you can develop a plan that defines:

- specific staffing requirements for the coming year
- the likely periods during the year when recruitment will be necessary.

Workforce planning does not mean that a vacancy that you had not anticipated will never occur. However, it should prevent the pressure that builds up in growing organizations when staff are required that have not been budgeted for. A well-considered workforce plan will have a positive impact on all your staff, and should enable you to predict the need to recruit new people throughout the year.

Recognizing the costs

Recruitment is expensive. Just consider some of the costs involved in terms of time and money:

- advertising costs
- agency costs
- developing an application form
- shortlisting applicants
- interviewing time by you
- interviewing time by your colleagues
- second interviews
- selection
- training and development.

It is easy to see why the planning stage of recruitment is actually the most important stage of all. Recruiting a member of staff who was not necessary, or appointing the wrong person, can cost you dearly. So spend as much time as you can spare considering:

- whether you need to recruit
- what specific role needs to be filled
- what sort of person you are looking for.

We will look at each of these issues in the coming chapters of this book.

Checklist

✓ Why has your vacancy arisen?
✓ Do you need to recruit?
✓ What are the alternatives?
✓ Does the job need to be full-time?
✓ Could someone else perform part/all of the role?
✓ Could you have predicted this vacancy?
✓ Do you have an overall workforce plan?
✓ Have you estimated the costs of recruiting?
✓ Do you *still* need to recruit?

02

analysing the job

In this chapter you will learn:

- how to put together a job description
- how to put together a person specification.

Now that you know for certain that you need to recruit, and you have considered all the alternatives, it is time to look at the position you need to fill, and the ideal person to fill it.

Reviewing the role

A thorough understanding and appraisal of the vacancy that you want to fill is absolutely vital to successful recruitment. Regardless of whether you are recruiting for a post that already exists, or for a completely new role, gathering information about it will help you to:

- compile a job description (outlining what the job holder will do)
- compile a person specification (summarizing the skills and attributes the ideal candidate is likely to have)
- put together an application form
- word a recruitment advertisement
- screen and interview candidates.

In short, if you do not understand the role that you are recruiting for, you are unlikely to appoint a suitable candidate.

So what type of information do you need to gather?

Information required

Your aim is to understand the role you are recruiting for in as much detail as you understand your own role. Use the following as a checklist for the type of information you need to gather in order to understand and appraise the role:

Purpose

Why are you recruiting at all? What is the main purpose of the role? See if you can summarize the role in a single sentence. Start by looking at the job title: Does it reflect the purpose of the role?

Principal objectives

Most roles have a number of distinct functions (e.g. Team member, customer service, sales). Some of these can be expressed as objectives (e.g. to achieve sales of £4000 per month). What are the principal objectives of the role?

Job type

Is this a full-time post? Could the role be performed part-time? Would a job share be appropriate? Think carefully about these questions, as the answers will provide a clear focus on the sort of person you are looking for.

Departments and colleagues

Who does the role report to? Which department will the new recruit work in? Will they have responsibility for staff themselves? Is the department a large one, or will the recruit be working in a small team? Will the recruit always be working as part of the team, or will a degree of self-sufficiency be required?

Physical location

Where will the job be based? Will travelling between sites be required? Will the recruit require a full driving licence? Is the department likely to move to a new location in the foreseeable future?

Prospects

Is there a recognized career path for the person recruited to this position? Is this a static or consistent role, which is unlikely to change much over time? This is an important issue: You will probably not want to recruit a ruthless and ambitious person to an unchanging or consistent role.

Authority/Responsibility

What authority or responsibility does the role carry? Does the role demand responsibility for other staff? For processes? For money? Will the person recruited to the role be required to hire or discipline staff? If so, you are looking for someone with specific experience and skills, which should narrow your search.

Assessment procedures

What monitoring and assessment procedures are currently in place for this role? Has the role developed in the past from the previous job holder's own skills, rather than the actual demands of the role? If so, now is the time to review the role before you start recruiting.

Skills and knowledge

What are the specific skills and knowledge requirements of the role? Does the role require someone with particular qualifications? Which of the skills are essential, and which are desirable?

Experience

What experience are you looking for in the candidate? Previous management or customer service experience? Perhaps no experience is required, and your organization will train the right candidate to perform the role. If so, think about how you might identify the *right* person.

You may find it helpful to summarize your analysis of the role in a single sheet of paper. If so, you will find the template on page 14 useful.

Sources of information

So where are you going to get all this information from? It is unlikely that you will have it all to hand. Every organization is different, but you will probably find most of the information you need from one of the following sources:

Existing job description

If the role already exists, does the existing job holder have a job description? If so, check it out, because it should provide important background on the purpose and objectives of the role. Give some thought to how much the role has changed or developed since this job description was compiled. Are the requirements of the role broadly the same now? If not, what has changed? A job vacancy is a great opportunity to revise and reconsider the role, so do not fall into the trap of automatically recruiting someone with exactly the same skills, knowledge and experience as the outgoing job holder.

Existing job holder

Many organizations now conduct exit interviews with the outgoing job holder to establish why they are leaving, and how their role has changed. The current job holder will know better than anyone the broad requirements of the role, as well as the frustrations and limitations that go with it. What did they do well? What did they spend more time on than they would have preferred doing? Consider whether the role needs to be redefined in light of how the existing job holder views it.

HEXHAM BAKERIES	
PROPOSED JOB TITLE	
DEPARTMENT/DIVISION	
MAIN PURPOSE OF ROLE	
MAIN TASKS AND RESPONSIBILITIES	
SKILLS KNOWLEDGE AND EXPERIENCE	
WORKING ENVIRONMENT	
PROSPECTS	
SALARY RANGE	
SIGNED	
NAME	
DATE	
POSITION	

job analysis template

Line manager

The line manager will have an opinion of the requirements of the role, and of the type of person they are looking for. They will also know the extent to which the role has developed in the past, and may have ideas about how the role could be redefined.

Organizational charts

If the organization publishes organizational charts of how departments, teams and team members fit in, these will help you to identify all the people that the recruit will come into contact with. You should quickly establish all the lines of communication required for the role.

Appraisal forms

If there is a formal appraisal system in your organization, the evidence of the existing job holder's appraisal forms will help you to see how the role has developed, as well as the specific training and development requirements of the role. You may also uncover evidence of relationships within the team or department that proved difficult. It is as well to know about these before you begin recruiting.

Personnel plans

Increasingly, organizations realize the importance and value of a highly motivated workforce. Your organization may already have been awarded IIP (Investors in People) status. Whether it has or not, you may have a personnel plan, which summarizes the organization's overall objectives and targets, the departments and individuals required to meet those objectives, and the specific training and development needs of those individuals. If such a document exists, remind yourself of the purpose of the department that has the vacancy, and the role of the member of the department that you are recruiting for.

Next steps

Having gathered all the information that you can about the role, consider it carefully, and ask yourself some important questions. In the light of what you now know about the role:

1 Are you sure that you still need to recruit?
2 Do you need to recruit for exactly the same position and role?
3 Do other team/department members duplicate the role?
4 Does the role need to be redefined?
5 Does the role require someone with the same skills and experience as the outgoing job holder?
6 Will the role continue to exist on the same terms?
7 Does the role demand a similar level of authority and responsibility?

Once you feel confident with the answers to all these questions, it is time to move on the next stage.

Compiling a job description

A job description is an essential tool in the recruitment process. At its most simple level, a job description outlines the main purpose, tasks and responsibilities of the position that you are trying to fill. Managers are often guilty of compiling a job description in a hurry or, worse, skipping this stage altogether. But compiling a job description will pay dividends because:

- it helps you to focus on the skills, knowledge and experience required to do the job
- it helps you to draft the wording used in the recruitment advertisement
- it can be sent out to prospective candidates, enabling them to decide whether or not they are qualified to do the job
- it will give you a tool against which to shortlist candidates
- you can use it to draw up a list of interview questions to ask each candidate
- you can refer to it during the interview to make sure that you have not missed something important.

Most important of all, you can use the job description, after you have appointed someone, to identify training and development needs, and refer to it during the appraisal process. Used properly, you will update a job description over time, in line with the changes and development of the role.

Tip
Even if this is not a new position, take time to bring the outgoing job holder's job description up to date. The role may have changed significantly since it was last updated.

If your organization takes training and development seriously, and has a training and development plan, you may find that there is a specific formula that all employees must follow when compiling a job description. If so, you must follow the formula, as a job description will be referred to during appraisal, grievance and discipline procedures, so it is vital that it is sufficiently robust, and matches your organization's needs.

If there is no company formula to follow, you may find the following short guide to job descriptions useful.

Simple job descriptions

A simple job description should summarize the basic requirements and conditions of the role. In most cases, you will probably be able to restrict this summary to a single sheet of paper. A simple job description should include the following.

Job title

Make sure that this is simple and unambiguous. Some companies often use titles that make jobs sound more important than they are. There is little to be gained from this, and it can often lead to confusion. So if you are recruiting for a junior role, advertise for a Sales Assistant, rather than a Sales Executive. Or Telephonist, rather than Customer Services Operative. You must make sure, however, that any job title that you use does not imply discrimination. Refer to Appendix on Discrimination (see page 199).

Job location

If the role requires travel, or working in several sites, then this should be stated. You may wish to keep all options open by stating that the role may require a move to another site at a later stage.

Who the job holder reports to

Use the line manager's title, rather than name. This will ensure that job descriptions always remain focused on roles, rather than the personality of the people performing those roles.

Job purpose, tasks and responsibilities

These should be listed simply and clearly. A basic job description will outline the key tasks and responsibilities only, to maintain the brevity of the document. This will also ensure that prospective candidates focus on their suitability to perform the most significant tasks of the role. Never use in-house or industry jargon to describe a task, and always spell out acronyms in full. For example, say *Sales Order Processing*, rather than *SOP*. The idea is to make a simple job description as clear and helpful as possible.

Hours required, grade and holiday entitlement

If the role demands normal office hours, then these should be stated. To some, this will mean 9.30 a.m. to 5.00 p.m. To you, it might mean 8.30 a.m. to 6.00 p.m. And build in some flexibility for working outside normal working hours on occasions. Perhaps you will need this person to work late when preparing for an annual sales conference, for example.

A job description that you have compiled should be signed and dated by you. This will indicate when the job description was last updated, and who compiled it. Opposite is a sample, basic job description that might assist you when compiling your own.

Tip

The most difficult sections to write are often the overall purpose of the job, and the principal duties. Try to summarize the principal duties before attempting to describe the overall purpose. If you identify the principal duties, you will find that they provide an ideal basis for encapsulating the main purpose of the job.

Tip

Try to use appropriate, well-chosen 'action' verbs to describe the key tasks and responsibilities. You may find the following list useful:

clerical	senior specialist	line management
check	analyse	plan
make available	proposed	direct
operate	interpret	establish
provide	advise	implement
maintain	appraise	achieve
submit	recommend	ensure
present	develop	maintain
		set
		review

PORTER COMMUNICATIONS LTD

Job Description

Job Title: Office Manager
Reporting to: Managing Director

Purpose of Job:
To manage the office, and the everyday administrative functions of the company. To manage the secretarial services provided, and to ensure an efficient customer service to clients and members of the public.

Principal Responsibilities:
1 Manage a team of eight secretarial and administrative staff with responsibility for word processing, filing, customer service, postal services, switchboard and reception.
2 Compile weekly staff schedules, and monthly statistical reports for senior management.
3 Manage systems for purchasing of office stationery and supplies, negotiating with local suppliers to ensure optimum value for money.
4 Supervise agency cleaning staff to ensure cleanliness and hygiene within all office areas.
5 Other administrative and secretarial services as required by the Managing Director from time to time.

Experience and Knowledge Requirements:
1 Substantial administrative experience and a proven track record in people management.
2 Excellent computing and word processing skills, as well as experience of telephone and switchboard systems.
3 Outstanding verbal and communication skills.
4 Education equivalent to two A Levels.

simple job description extract

Longer job descriptions

Many organizations use job descriptions for ongoing appraisal of the job holder, as well as for the initial recruitment and selection process. If this is the case in your organization, then the simple, one-page job descriptions are unlikely to be sufficient.

For appraisal purposes you really need a job description that lists not only the key responsibilities, but also the individual objectives and tasks that make up each responsibility. For example, let's look at the role of an editor in a publishing company. The principal task might be to monitor the stock and financial performance of a series of books. In a simple job description, the responsibility would be listed simply as:

Key Responsibility
- Monitor the stock and financial performance of the DIY Gardening Series

---

But when it comes to the appraisal, how will you judge whether this task has been completed satisfactorily or not? Is it enough to monitor stock levels once a year? Once a month? Once each day? Is there a minimum stock level that must be maintained at all times? Is there a maximum stock value that must not be exceeded?

A longer job description provides clarification for each responsibility, ensuring that the role can be appraised at any time in a fair and unambiguous way. So, the example above might look like this:

Key Responsibility
- Monitor the stock and financial performance of the DIY Gardening Series
  - monitor stock levels on a weekly basis
  - agree reprint quantities with Publishing Director
  - ensure appropriate text corrections are made
  - arrange reprint with Production Manager
  - inform customer services department and marketing team of schedules.

Check the following at least monthly:
  - sales performance of list
  - ongoing editorial and production costs.

Report monthly to Publishing Director on sales and costs.

You need to think carefully about whether to spend time developing a longer job description for the role that you are recruiting for. There is no doubt that such a job description would assist both the recruitment and ongoing assessment of the job holder. But they can be very challenging to write. It is not always possible to define, in simple terms, the tasks that make up every responsibility. Even if you can, a job description is likely to be several pages long.

Ultimately, the type of job description you use may be directed by the environment and culture of the organization that you work for. However, whether you use the shorter or longer format, a clear, unambiguous job description is an essential tool in the recruitment and selection process, and you should allow time to compile one as thoroughly as you can (see page 22).

Person specification

So far we have looked at the ways that a job description summarizes the role, key tasks and responsibilities of the vacancy. The next factor to consider is the type of person that would best perform that role.

A person specification is a document that sets out the skills, knowledge and experience required to do the job properly.

A well-thought-out person specification will assist the recruitment process:

- useful when wording the recruitment advertisement
- provides guidance on where to recruit
- guidance for questions to ask on job application form
- useful checklist when shortlisting candidates
- ideal for planning the questions to ask at interview
- can help to identify appropriate selection tests for shortlisted candidates
- assists with training and development after candidate has been selected.

In fact, a person specification, used alongside the job description, provides the ideal platform for all stages of the recruitment process.

While it is a good idea to provide applicants with a copy of the job description, it is better to retain the person specification for your own use because potential candidates, armed with the

Marketing Assistant

1 Introduction

The main focus of the Marketing Assistant's role is to provide support and information to the sales and marketing function. The Marketing Assistant reports to the Sales & Marketing Director, but also supports the Customer Services Manager and the Home Sales Manager. The Marketing Assistant is expected to manage his/her own agenda, within a framework set by the Sales & Marketing Director.

Areas of responsibility

Communication

Routine information provision between the marketing department and other departments within the company, between the company and its trade sales force, between the company and its UK trade customers, and between the company and its overseas customers, agents and distributors world-wide.

Detailed breakdown

1.1 Compile and distribute amongst all staff short weekly memos outlining the campaigns that the marketing department is currently engaged in using information provided by Departmental Managers.

1.2 Provide weekly memos for the trade sales force, and ad hoc reports as requested by the Home Sales Manager using information provided by the Customer Services Manager.

1.3 Update trade customers with details of new products and services using information provided by Departmental Managers and the Customer Services Manager.

1.4 Provide monthly product release schedules to Trade Representatives.

1.5 Provide printouts for Trade Representatives as requested, and information from the customer database as requested by the Home Sales Manager.

1.6 Compile and distribute a monthly memo of other relevant information for Trade Representatives using information provided by the Customer Services Manager and the Home Sales Manager.

1.7 Ensure that sample products are sent to the trade sales force, trade customers, and overseas agents and distributors.

1.8 Compile and distribute a composite memo by the tenth of each month to all agents and distributors world-wide using information provided by Departmental Managers and the Customer Services Manager.

1.9 Proof-read all promotional literature generated by Marketing Department.

longer job description extract

person specification, can simply pretend to be exactly the person you are looking for, and frame their answers accordingly.

Content

So what should a person specification look like? As with job descriptions, your organization may already have a preferred style and approach. If so, you should follow it. If not, you may find the following guidance helpful.

Although a person specification may vary between organizations, and from job to job, the process of compiling one will almost invariably be the same. The place to start is the job description. You have already summarized what is required of the role: the key tasks, the objectives and the responsibilities. Now you must consider carefully the likely skills, knowledge and qualifications required to fulfil them. What might the ideal candidate be like?

For example, if you need to recruit a manager for a busy call centre, you are obviously going to be looking for someone who can handle pressure, who can motivate a team, and who probably has management experience. These would all be listed in the person specification.

Typically, the person specification would be divided into a number of different headings.

Qualifications

What professional qualifications would the ideal candidate possess? What level of education are you looking for?

You need to be careful with this section of the person specification. Education is going through a great deal of change. Employers argue that a degree from one university is not as rigorous as one from another. There is a lot of discussion in the media about how much easier A Levels are these days. Start by listing the minimum qualifications required to do the job, and then add desirable additional qualifications where appropriate. Do not be tempted to employ an overqualified candidate, who might become bored very quickly and leave. Similarly, an underqualified candidate might simply not be able to do the job.

If you are unsure of the specific qualifications that may be required for the role, list instead the specific knowledge needed. This will give you an easy way to filter candidates during the recruitment process.

Skills and abilities

What specific skills or abilities would the ideal candidate possess?

Will the ideal person need to be a self-starter, a team-member, or both? Will they need to negotiate keenly with suppliers? What about giving presentations? Or solving problems? Does the role involve precision/manual dexterity?

Don't hold back at this stage. Imagine that you have the perfect candidate sitting in front of you. What skills and abilities would they have?

Experience

Experience is another area where you should apply caution. It is tempting to employ someone with several years' experience in a similar role, because you might feel that they would require less training, and would fit into the new role more quickly.

However, be realistic. Some jobs require no experience at all, whilst others require both qualified and experienced staff. Someone who has performed a similar role for many years might be looking for a new challenge, and would quickly become bored doing the same job for a different organization.

Remember that the ability to do a job should not just be measured in terms of the number of years' experience that an applicant has. Someone with wider, rather than longer, experience may be more useful to you.

Finally, don't be greedy! There is no need to employ a maths graduate to count pallets in the warehouse, or a qualified marketer to join as Junior Marketing Executive. Think in terms of the experience that you think the role demands.

Personality

It can be hard to put in words the ideal candidate's personality traits, but it can also be very revealing.

Does the role involve a degree of pressure? For example, sales roles often have targets and deadlines that must be met. If it does, then you are looking for someone who handles pressure well, and who appears confident at interview.

Many roles demand patience. For example, checking that deliveries arrive complete and undamaged, or repetitive tasks like product assembly.

Many roles involve a high level of decision making. We often hear about organizations and departments where nothing gets done because the manager seems incapable of making a decision.

Think creatively about the ideal candidate. Summarize their personality characteristics. Don't worry at this stage if you think that such a person couldn't possibly exist.

Physical characteristics

Your person specification should consider several physical characteristics.

What would the ideal candidate's general appearance be like? If, for example, they would regularly meet customers, you would want them to be articulate and presentable. If the role was mainly office bound, this would be less relevant.

What about their health? For example, does the role require a minimum level of eyesight or hearing? What about physical ability? Does the job demand a particularly strong or able-bodied person?

List the physical requirements of the role in the person specification. Be as objective and flexible as possible. Make absolutely certain that you are not discriminating on grounds of age, sex or disability.

Style

If you have worked through this section, you probably have quite a long list of skills and attributes that you are looking for in your candidate. Before putting your person specification to use, there are two things you can do to make your document more useful.

First, read through the list once more. For each skill or attribute, decide whether it is *essential* that the successful applicant possesses it, or *desirable*. Mark each entry with an 'e' for essential or a 'd' for desirable. This step will speed up the shortlisting process dramatically. If a clean driving licence is an essential skill for the role, you may legitimately reject all applicants who do not have one. You might also want to rank the attributes required in order of importance for the role.

Second, you may wish to review your list once more, and ensure that the skills and attributes described are clearly expressed, precise and unambiguous. Be sure that you have read and understood the requirements of current discrimination legislation, and that your list is fair, honest and, above all, legal.

You will find a sample person specification overleaf.

PERSON SPECIFICATION
JOB TITLE: Office Administrator, St Peter's School

Those categories marked 'E', for essential, will be used especially for the purpose of shortlisting.

1. Job-related knowledge/aptitude/skills

Knowledge:
Of office procedures **E**
Of word processing **E**

Aptitude:
Able to demonstrate a commitment to the delivery of high quality education
Able to understand the needs of pupils (and their parents)
Able to understand the need for and maintain confidentiality

Skills:
Able to deal professionally with staff, parents, visitors and external organizations
Word processing (min 35wpm to be tested)
Numeracy and communication skills
Organized approach to work
Able to prioritize work and manage time

2. Experience
Working unsupervised **E**
Working as part of a team **E**
Providing a confidential secretarial service **E**
Delivering a range of high quality administrative services **E**
Using word processing, spreadsheets and database packages **E**

3. General education
No specific requirement

4. Personal qualities
Able to react calmly under pressure
Reliable and conscientious
Flexible attitude to work

5. Circumstances
Able to attend evening meetings occasionally and work late if required

6. Physical
No specific requirement

7. Equal opportunities
An awareness of equal opportunities issues **E**
A commitment to implement the Centre's Equal Opportunities Policy **E**

sample person specification

Checklist

✓ Do you understand fully the requirements and responsibilities of the position you need to fill?

✓ Could you describe why this role is important to the organization, and how it relates to other team or department roles?

✓ Have you compiled a job description for the role?

✓ Have you considered what skills, knowledge and experience the ideal candidate is likely to have?

✓ Have you put together a person specification?

03 establishing the terms of employment

In this chapter you will learn:

- about the types of vacancy that exist
- about the alternatives to looking for a full-time member of staff
- how to set a salary range and scale.

Now that you have considered the roles and responsibilities of the job, and the type of person you are looking for, it is time to consider the main terms and conditions of the position.

Part-time or full-time?

Whether the position you are recruiting for is a new one, or you are recruiting to replace someone who has left your organization, it is a good idea to consider carefully the terms of employment that you can offer. In the first place, ask yourself whether the position requires a full-time employee, or if someone working part-time could perform the role. There are two main factors to consider:

The amount of work

Does the volume of work demand a full-time employee? Could someone working three days each week perform the role effectively? Has the role been performed by a full- or part-time person until now? If this is undoubtedly a role requiring five days each week, then recruiting someone full-time is really the only option.

The intensity of work

Some roles are particularly demanding at certain times of the day, like lunch periods, or first thing each morning. Examples include customer service positions, or catering roles. If the vacancy you wish to fill falls into this category, then it is a good idea to consider recruiting someone part-time. There are several advantages to employing one or more part-time staff.

Advantages of part-time staff

1 Part-time staff tend to be more flexible about the hours that they can work. They can cover peak periods such as lunch hours, or when the phone lines are particularly busy.

2 Employing a number of part-time staff increases your ability to cover sickness, holidays and other absences.

3 Many part-time staff are happy to increase their working hours when trade picks up, or as the demands of the job dictate.

4 During busy periods, you can usually pay part-time staff at their hourly rate, rather than paying overtime to full-time employees.

Disadvantages of part-time staff

1 You may find it harder to recruit part-time staff. Although part-time work suits many applicants, the majority of job hunters will be looking for full-time positions. You can assume that it will take as long to recruit and train a part-time employee as it does a full-time one.

2 You need to establish any other commitments that the potential part-time employee might have. Do they work anywhere else? What hours do they work for another employer? You may discover that your part-time employee is not as flexible as you imagined.

Short-term contracts

You may have decided that you need to recruit a full-time employee, but this does not mean that the position has to be a permanent one. Offering a short-term contract allows you to recruit someone to fill a role for a fixed period, often for six or twelve months.

When considering whether a short-term contract is appropriate, ask yourself the following questions:

1 Is it likely that the role will exist, in its current form, for more than a year?

2 Does the role exist as a result of a short-term or long-term increase in sales or performance?

3 If the employee left in two years' time, would you be likely to replace them?

4 Are the skills or knowledge required for the role difficult to find?

5 Might technology or machinery develop over the next two years, such that the role will no longer exist?

6 Are you recruiting to cover another employee during absence (long-term sickness or maternity leave)?

If you are in doubt about the longevity of the role, you should consider employing someone on a short-term contract. If you recruit a good employee, and they are motivated to stay with your organization, then they may accept a permanent contract at a later date.

If a position is proving particularly difficult to fill, or you are not entirely sure about what the role might eventually entail, then it can be beneficial to employ someone on a short-term contract initially, until a permanent solution can be found. You can re-employ your recruit on a permanent basis if they perform well, or you can recruit someone else.

There are dangers associated with short-term contracts, however. Your recruit may continue to look for a permanent position after you have employed them, and may not last the duration of the contract. During the last few weeks or months of the contract, your employee's attention may be more focused on finding another job, rather than on performing well for your organization. You cannot always expect the same commitment from an employee on a short-term contract as from a permanent employee.

Nevertheless, short-term contracts may be the solution in your particular case. Good recruitment involves considering every option available.

Job sharing

Job sharing is when two people share responsibility for a role or for achieving certain objectives. The two employees are jointly answerable to their line manager, and often work on separate days to combine to make up a full-time position. In the UK, it is becoming more common to offer positions to job sharers, and employers are starting to recognize the many advantages that they bring to an organization.

Employers often complain that they lose good employees because their circumstances change such that they are no longer able to work full-time. If the demands of the role dictate that it would not suit a part-time employee, then the employer often loses a good member of staff. Job sharing can provide the answer.

Some organizations welcome applications from candidates looking for a job share, and will refer to this in the recruitment advertisement. Others do not actively encourage it, but are happy to consider it if the right candidate(s) apply. Job sharing often suits female staff returning from maternity leave, who would otherwise think twice about returning full-time. There are a number of situations that suit job sharing, and you should be open to the idea when planning your recruitment campaign.

If you need to recruit for a role that requires several key, though not complementary, skills, then job sharing can provide the perfect solution. For example, if you are looking for someone with management and administrative skills, you may find the search easier if you are able to split the role and recruit two job sharers, each with experience of one of the skills you are looking for.

Organizations offering job sharing opportunities tend to offer the same terms, pay and conditions to each of the job sharers. But you do not have to follow this model. You could split the role between a senior member of staff and a more junior one, for example. The senior job sharer could be involved in training the junior one, perhaps with an eye to taking on the role full-time in the future.

There is a danger associated with splitting responsibility for a role between two people. You need to ensure that the job sharers understand that they are equally culpable, and share responsibility for the role between them. You also need to encourage every possible means of communication between them. If the job sharers are never in the office on the same days, you need to establish regular telephone, e-mail or face-to-face contact between them.

Using freelancers

Freelancers are self-employed workers that you can call upon, when you need them, to perform specific finite tasks for your organization. You should consider using a freelancer when:

- the role that you are recruiting is finite, and contains specific targets or objectives
- the position is likely to be redundant in the foreseeable future
- the role does not demand a full-time employee, and the position is not appropriate for a part-timer
- the role could be performed on- or off-site
- the role could change significantly over time
- there is insufficient budget for a full-time employee
- the role exists as a result of a short-term increase in sales or performance.

Freelancers are often used as an alternative to offering a fixed short-term contract. A freelancer carries few overheads for the organization, and will not appear on its staff list or salary costs. Although a freelancer's daily rate will be higher than a salaried member of staff, you need employ them only to undertake specific tasks when you need them. Over a six-month period, therefore, they cost an organization less than a salaried member of staff.

Freelancers are often used to provide skilled services that the organization does not have in-house, like graphic design, public relations, copywriting or training. Freelance staff are not always the answer, but they do allow an organization to call upon expert staff as and when they need them.

Finding freelancers

Throughout the recession of the 1990s, UK companies made thousands of staff redundant, only to re-employ many of them on a freelance basis. The result is that there is a vast reserve of competent, skilled freelancers in the UK for virtually any role that your organization needs to perform. But where and how will you find them?

You may find that you have ex-staff who are now self-employed in a similar field. If you don't, it is worth asking colleagues and staff if they know anyone working in the particular field you are looking for. You would be surprised how many leads you will generate.

Freelancers are responsible for marketing and selling themselves, so there are several other methods for locating the right one for you. If you are computer literate then the internet can greatly assist your search.

Internet searches

If you type 'freelance' together with the type of vacancy that you have (like 'sales' or 'graphic design') into one of the better search engines, you will find a number of freelance individuals and groups that should satisfy your criteria. Search engines tend to give mixed results, however, and you may want to go for a more targeted search.

There are a number of websites dedicated to finding work for freelancers, and to putting organizations in touch with them. One of the most popular is www.elance.com. Here, freelancers can enter their details, experience, qualifications and references into a searchable, categorized database. Potential employers can search the database for the freelancer most suitable for the work on offer. The site has a useful category listing (Accounting & Finance, Administration, Business Strategy, Graphic Design, Legal, etc.), or a search engine to enter a more specific keyword string.

There are other freelance network websites that cater for specific industries or functions. www.freelancers.net, for example, offers a comprehensive network site for freelancers in the web design and IT industry. If you have a website project, or need some programming code to be written, this would be an excellent way to locate freelance staff, bypassing expensive web-building design agencies.

However you locate the freelance staff that you employ, make sure that you give them a tight and well-defined brief. Issue them with a contract, and manage their work as if they were salaried staff.

Salary ranges and scales

Before you start the recruitment process, you need to have considered the important issue of what you will pay. Larger organizations often have comprehensive salary bands and scales in place, with a fixed upper and lower salary for each type of role. These are generally reviewed annually, and are based on some of the following factors:

- the level of responsibility of the role
- the contribution of the role towards sales or profit goals
- the skills and experience required for the role.

Notice how these factors are all based on the role itself, rather than on the person performing it. If you work for a larger organization that has salary bands and scales in place, then the job of deciding what you will pay may be a straightforward one. If your organization does not have a fixed salary system, then the answers to the following questions should help you to determine what you will have to offer potential employees:

1 What was the outgoing job holder's salary?
2 Did the issue of salary contribute to the departure of the outgoing job holder?
3 How important is this role to the objectives of the department/team/organization?
4 What level of responsibility does the role carry?
5 What skills/experience are you looking for?
6 Are these skills/experience hard to find?
7 What do your competitors pay for similar roles?
8 What salaries are offered in classified advertisements for similar roles?

9 What do trade/professional associations recommend for this type of role?

If you cannot answer all of the questions above, then consider doing a bit of research. Ask colleagues both inside and outside your organization. Contact the relevant professional associations, if they exist. Ask a recruitment agency for advice. With a little networking and simple research, you should have a feel for what is the 'going rate'.

Pay the 'staying rate' not the 'going rate'!

A very successful businessman once gave me this simple piece of advice. If you want to recruit motivated, loyal employees, then you should pay the 'staying rate' not the 'going rate'. In other words, the 'going rate' is what everyone else pays. That's fine, if the skills required are easy to find. But recruitment is an expensive business. An employee can leave an organization for many reasons. By paying a little more than the 'going rate' you will ensure that an employee leaves for a reason beyond your control, rather than just to work for your competitor for a higher salary.

Consider an upper and lower salary band that is fair, and that will encourage the most skilled or able to apply. You do not have to advertise the salary during the recruitment process, unless you want to, but be prepared to discuss it if asked. Above all, remain flexible. You might wish to take on someone more junior than you had originally planned, in which case you can offer a lower salary, combined with an appropriate training package. Or you might find yourself taking on someone more skilled than you had expected, in which case you will probably have to offer a higher salary.

Checklist

✓ Are you looking for a part-time or full-time employee?
✓ Should you offer a short-term contract?
✓ Is the role suitable for job sharing?
✓ Would using freelancers be effective?
✓ What salary range and scale will you offer?

part two

attracting applicants

04

recruiting internally

In this chapter you will learn:

- how to recruit from inside your organization
- how to advertise internally
- how to reject internal candidates.

By now you should know what sort of person you are looking for. The question you need to address now is where will you find them? Before you spend money on advertising the vacancy externally, have a look around you. Your new recruit may already be working within your organization.

Transfers and promotions

If your organization has a personnel plan or a formal appraisal system in place, you are probably aware of:

- current staffing levels
- current staffing requirements
- anticipated staffing requirements for the next 12 months
- employees with potential for transfer or promotion.

Some companies will provide good employees with training and development in anticipation of future prospects and promotion opportunities. Even if you do not have a formal personnel plan, you may still have the ideal recruit from amongst your existing workforce. There are a number of advantages to promoting or transferring existing staff:

1 You already know how an existing employee works, their strengths and weaknesses, their training and development needs, their performance, and their loyalty and commitment.
2 Existing staff have already adapted to the organization's culture and working style.
3 You will save time and expense on external recruitment.
4 It is motivating, both for the promoted employee and for other staff, to work for an organization that is seen to promote from within.

But there are challenges to overcome as well:

1 You must always recruit the person most suited to the role, not necessarily the person who is 'next in line'. This can lead to dissatisfied employees who consider that they have been overlooked.
2 You still have to go through a thorough, formal and fair recruitment procedure, giving others the chance to apply for the vacancy.
3 You need to strike a balance between the need to retain good employees and the need to bring fresh, new ideas and thinking into the organization.

Tip
No candidate, internal or external, is likely to be perfectly experienced and qualified for the role you are recruiting for. Weigh up the
costs and time involved in training and developing an existing
employee, against advertising, selecting and appointing an external candidate. Don't forget that external candidates will probably
need training and development themselves.

Advertising internally

Your ideal candidate may already work for your organization. If
yours is a large organization, with hundreds or thousands of
employees, there may be someone working for another division
or department who is already looking for another job. So how
do you make sure that you attract their attention?

- notice boards and bulletin boards
- company newsletters
- internal e-mail
- company intranet
- memos and circulars
- direct approaches.

If you go for the direct approach, make sure that you are being
fair to all potential applicants. Office gossip will ensure that the
word is spread about a vacancy, so make sure that you exploit
this.

Rejecting internal candidates

When an internal applicant is rejected for an internally advertised position, you are likely to create a disgruntled employee.
Sometimes this can affect the candidate's morale and confidence
so badly that they feel forced to leave the organization altogether.
So it is important to take time to explain why they were rejected
for the role, what specific skills or attributes were missing, and
what the candidate could do to ensure that they would be successful next time. Your aim is to ensure that they are not dis-
couraged to apply for other internal vacancies in the future. You
may wish to discuss specific training that the candidate should
consider in order to be better suited for a role of the type you are
recruiting for.

Turning temporary staff into permanent staff

This is a little-used method of recruitment that can be extremely effective. You can turn temporary staff to permanent staff in one of two ways:

1 If you already employ a number of temporary or casual staff, you can search from amongst them for someone suitable for the vacancy.
2 You can recruit a temporary member of staff to fill the vacancy, and then see if they are suitable for permanent employment.

Although either of these methods can work, the second method involves two main hazards. First, you will be charged heavily by the recruitment agency that supplied you with the temporary member of staff if you offer them a permanent position. Second, you may find the ideal employee, but they may not be looking for something permanent.

Trawling through your temporary staff is good practice, however. People take on temporary work for a number of reasons, and some might be only too glad to have the security offered by a permanent position. Others might be willing to juggle their other commitments in order to work for you full-time.

Case study

Joe was studying for a business degree part-time (mainly evenings) at a London university. He took on temporary work helping out the busy customer service department of a publishing company during his summer recess. Although the work was initially for August only, the company asked him to work in September and October as well, to cover their autumn sales season. Joe found that he could work three days each week without affecting his studying time. When the company was looking for a full-time Marketing Assistant, Joe seemed ideally suited to the role. When the Marketing Director discussed the vacancy with him, Joe was concerned that he would not have sufficient time left to study. With a little negotiation, the Marketing Director and Joe reached a compromise that satisfied both parties. Joe would work a 35-hour week, leaving him with enough time to study in the evenings and at weekends. Joe was delighted to find an employer prepared to be flexible throughout his period of study.

He was also glad about the prospects that working for the company would offer. The Marketing Director was delighted to have appointed someone whose work she knew, and whose commitment was already proven.

Retirees

Workers approaching retirement are often interested in staying on in an organization on a part-time basis, or in returning as an independent consultant or contractor. It may be because they need the money, but more often it is because they find the prospect of so much free time daunting. Either way, using a retiree to close your vacancy gap can be very sensible.

- their work/attendance record is known to you
- they will probably require less training/induction
- they already understand the work ethic and culture.

Of course, in most organizations, the chances of finding just the right candidate, just as they are approaching retirement, are slim. But if the outgoing job holder is retiring, consider whether they might want to stay on part-time, or continue part of or all the role as an independent contractor.

Former employees

Some companies have a policy not to re-employ staff who have left them, unless they left on health or maternity grounds. If your organization has such a policy, then this section is not relevant to you.

For everyone else, how would you feel about re-employing a former member of staff? Usually, the answer lies in the reasons that they left in the first place. Clearly, if you had to dismiss the staff member, there is no question of offering them another position. But what if they left to work for one of your competitors? Your pride might tell you not to consider them. However, they may have gained useful market knowledge from having worked at two companies in the same sector, which makes them very desirable.

Don't feel embarrassed to contact a former employee to see how happy they are in their new position. They may regret having left your organization, and be only too pleased to return. Keep all your options open. You have no obligation to re-employ a former employee, but you should not rule out the possibility either.

Often, an employee cites the lack of opportunity as the reason for leaving. If you now have such an opportunity available, then it is certainly worth making contact to discuss the position. They may be pleased to return to a position with better prospects and greater opportunity. If they do not, you can still ask them if they know someone else who might be right for the position. This can often lead to a referral, and so it is worth making contact.

Referrals

When recruiting new staff, some organizations ask their own staff for referrals. If they recruit someone who has been recommended by a member of staff, then the organization will reward that staff member. The rationale is straightforward. Your staff know what it is like to work for your organization. They know and understand the terms and conditions, as well as the culture and working environment. If they are motivated in the organization, then it is likely that some of their friends or associates might be as well. Besides, they are hardly likely to recommend that a friend joins an organization that will not suit them, are they?

If you decide to ask your existing staff for a referral, you must make several points absolutely clear:

1 Their application will be considered in the same way as any other applicant.
2 They must apply in the appropriate fashion, either by application form, or by covering letter with CV.
3 They will not be guaranteed an interview. They will be short-listed only on merit.
4 They will require references other than the existing member of staff.

Drop-ins

If your organization is based in a town or central location, you may find that people drop in from time to time to see if there are any job vacancies. They will often leave a copy of their CV with you. It makes sense to keep these CVs on file for a fixed period of time, in case a suitable position presents itself. If you have such a system in place, it is worth reviewing the CVs of these candidates before committing to recruiting externally.

Checklist

✓ Is there someone in your organization who you would consider transferring or promoting?

✓ Where might you advertise internally?

✓ How would you handle having to reject internal candidates?

✓ Do you have suitable temporary staff who might be interested in a permanent position?

✓ Has the retirement of a staff member created the vacancy? Would the person be willing or able to continue some or all of the role part-time?

✓ Would you consider appointing a former employee?

✓ Do any of your existing staff know of a friend or colleague who might be suitable for the role?

✓ Could you introduce a reward programme for staff referrals?

05

using agencies and headhunters

In this chapter you will learn:

- how to find the right agency
- how to brief them effectively
- what agencies and headhunters cost.

If you have exhausted the possibilities of recruiting internally, it is time to look outside the organization. Recruitment agencies and headhunters provide a range of professional services that might suit your needs ideally.

Specialist agencies

Recruitment agencies are known by a number of different names, although in essence they perform the same broad functions.

Many recruitment agencies are industry or function specialists. This means that they have specific experience of recruiting for specific types of organization (for example, legal, accountancy or childcare organizations) or particular job types (for example, secretarial, administrative or teaching roles). Although they will still need careful briefing, they may well understand how organizations like yours work, and appreciate many of the technical and personality requirements of the role that you are recruiting for.

Agencies come into their own because of the experience and systems that they already have in place. If you are trying to fill a vacancy on your own, you may be starting from scratch. You might have a few leads to follow up, or know of a good journal to place an advertisement in, but apart from these you are a little lost. A good recruitment agency, however, will have an up-to-date database of candidates who are looking for new positions, and who might be ideally suited to your position. An experienced agency will have met many of these candidates personally, and could put together a shortlist of suitable candidates at short notice.

Interviewing experience

An established recruitment agency will have interviewed thousands of candidates for hundreds of jobs, and so will be knowledgeable and experienced about the types of questions to ask at interview, and how to ask them. Organizations often use agencies to conduct the first round of interviews, and only get involved once the agency has selected a shortlist of suitable candidates.

Industry knowledge

It may sound obvious, but recruitment agencies know how to recruit staff! They:

- understand how and where to advertise (indeed, they may have already block-booked the best spaces in the trade media)
- know how to design and place an eye-catching recruitment advertisement
- know how to assess a CV, as well as see beyond it
- know how best to draw up a shortlist of candidates to interview
- have years of experience of interviewing prospective candidates.

Briefing the agency

No matter how experienced the agency, or how confidently you believe that they are right for you, it is essential to brief them as fully as you can. Using an agency is extremely expensive, and you are throwing money away if you do not spend time with an agency representative at the beginning, giving them as much information as you can about the role that you need to fill, and the type of person that you think could fill it.

Start with a thorough specification of the role. Give the agency a copy of the job description and person specification. Your contact at the agency should understand all the responsibilities of the role, as well as the personality factors that will influence your ultimate selection of a candidate.

They should also understand which factors are essential, which are important, and which are desirable. It is unlikely that any agency will find a person that matches every single one of your requirements, so you need the agency to appreciate which factors are more important than others. For example, some requirements of the role may be essential (like a clean driving licence), whilst others may be desirable (like a professional qualification).

Briefing an agency properly is a time-consuming process. However, it is time extremely well spent. It will ensure that the agency only puts forward candidates that are closely matched to your person specification, and who are likely to fit in to your organization. So it is better to spend time briefing the agency properly, than to waste time interviewing unsuitable candidates put forward by an agency that has been poorly briefed.

Once you have established a relationship with a recruitment agency, it makes sense to evaluate periodically how effective it has been as a recruiting source. For each vacancy, record the number of referrals made by the agency, as well as the number of people employed as a direct result of these referrals. If there are few referrals, or a low conversion rate between referrals and hires, you should re-evaluate the relationship with the agency.

You might conclude that the agency did not really understand the specifications of the job you were trying to fill. Perhaps spending time improving the communication between you and the agency will make future recruitment drives more effective. However, it might be that this was not the right agency to use for this particular position. The agency might perform admirably when recruiting for administrative or secretarial positions, but does not have the experience or expertise for managerial or technical positions. Make sure that you also evaluate the performance of the agency with reference to the state of the job market as a whole. Is this a particularly difficult time to recruit in general? Is there a shortage of people in the particular field in which you are trying to recruit? If the job market itself is unstable, then it would be harsh to blame an agency for not producing the ideal candidate.

Exclusivity

Some organizations use several agencies at a time when recruiting. After all, why not have two agencies looking for your ideal candidate and so reduce the overall time it takes to fill the vacancy? Well, there are pitfalls associated with using multiple agencies, and it is rarely to be recommended.

In a specialist field, for example, two or more agencies may put forward the same candidate. If this happens, it is your responsibility to credit the first agency who brought this person to your attention. It is good practice to date-stamp each application as it arrives to make sure that you know which agency sent each application, and when they sent it. You will find that most agencies are unwilling to work on anything other than an exclusive basis. It usually works best if you engage the services of an agency on an exclusive basis, but for a limited period only. After, say, three weeks, you could review the situation with the agency, and brief another agency if you feel it appropriate.

Choosing the right agency

So where do you start in your hunt for the perfect recruitment agency?

You may not have to look very hard at all. Some agencies are very active in promoting themselves, and may already have contacted you on a number of occasions introducing their services to you. If not, they may have approached one or more of your colleagues, and so it is a good idea to talk with them about any agencies that they may know. If your organization has a personnel department, they may have details of a number of agencies they have used successfully in the past.

If you are starting your hunt for an agency from scratch, the first place to try is the newspapers. Start locally. If you look through the jobs pages in the local newspaper, you are likely to see a number of vacancies advertised by the same organization. These advertisements will have been placed by an agency, which is advertising a number of positions on behalf of the organizations that the agency currently represents. Look through the vacancies on offer, and see if there are similar positions being advertised to your own. You should be able to identify the specialist areas of each agency. For example, some agencies tend to recruit for general or administrative positions only. Other agencies specialize in a particular field, such as publishing or marketing. If you see an agency that fits the profile you are looking for, take down their details and contact them.

If you know that the position you need to fill is likely to need a national search, start with the national press. Take a look through the classified advertisements of a newspaper that advertises jobs similar to yours, and record details of appropriate agencies. If you are struggling to find what you are looking for in the national press, consider trade journals and professional magazines that are published for your industry. Many of these have job sections, where specialist agencies often advertise their current positions.

The important issue is to ensure that you select an agency that is appropriate for the position that you are recruiting for. There is no point in engaging the services of a highly regarded agency if they do not have the expertise to recruit for your particular needs. If the vacancy you need to fill is an administrative assistant, then use a general or clerical agency. If the position is specialist, then find an agency with industry-specific expertise.

Finding the names of experienced agencies is only part of the job. An agency is only as good as the people who work for it. You must make sure that you meet the particular agency staff who will be dealing with your recruitment issue. Interview them, as you would a potential employee. Remember that they will effectively be representing your organization during the recruitment process. Do they share, or at least understand, your organization's culture? Do they understand your specific needs? Are they qualified to recruit for this position? Do they understand the specific requirements of the role?

Just as when recruiting a member of staff, you should take references and follow them up. Talk to another organization that has used this agency. What was their experience?

You can often get a feel for how the agency works by visiting it in person. Check to see how busy the agency feels on the day that you visit. Were you greeted politely? What impression did you get about the agency staff and surroundings? Was the office presentable?

Agency feedback

Providing feedback to an agency is just as important as briefing it in the first place. You should contact the agency after every interview, to review your reaction to each applicant with your contact. If the candidate is not suitable for the role, explain the reasons why so that your contact can make a better selection next time. This might sound obvious, but if you fail to take this simple step, you should not be surprised if the agency continues to put forward unsuitable candidates. The more feedback you provide, the more suitable the next candidate put forward by the agency will be.

Equally, if you plan to take a candidate forward to the next stage, explain to the contact what you like about them and why you think they might be suitable for the role. As soon as you feel you have seen a sufficient number of candidates from which to select, let the agency know. They will have built up relationships with their candidates, and so will not want to put forward candidates for a role that is likely to have been filled.

Working with an agency can be time-consuming, but the effort of building an effective relationship will pay dividends.

Agency costs

For full-time positions, most agencies charge a percentage of the annual salary paid to the employee. The actual percentage charge usually varies according to the salary paid. On average, you might expect to pay a fee of 10 per cent of the first year's annual salary. But this percentage might rise the higher the annual salary. It is therefore worth shopping around when considering which agency to use, as fees will vary between agencies. If you are looking to recruit a part-time employee, you may find that the agency is willing to negotiate a flat fee for finding the right candidate, rather than a percentage of the salary paid.

When weighing up the cost of using an agency, consider all the elements involved. Remember that there are rarely any upfront costs. You only pay a fee if a person referred by the agency is appointed to the position that you are trying to fill. You should also note that this fee is refundable, or at least partly refundable, if the candidate proves to be unsuitable within the first month or so of employment. If the employee leaves, or is dismissed, during the first month, the refund is often 100 per cent. During the second or third month, the refund can be 75 per cent. During the fourth, fifth or sixth months, it can be 50 per cent. Some agencies choose not to refund money. Instead, they may offer to find another candidate to fill the vacancy for no additional fee.

Although agency fees appear high, bear in mind that the costs of advertising, selecting and interviewing a number of applicants can be considerably higher than the agency fee. Since the agency only puts forward pre-screened applicants, you save both time and money, making the recruitment process cost-effective.

Every agency works in a slightly different way. Before you deal with a new agency, ensure that you see a written statement of their fee structure, refund policy and working practice, so that there will be no misunderstanding at a later stage.

Headhunters and what they do

If your organization is recruiting for a senior position, you may find it necessary to approach a headhunter. Headhunters, or executive search consultants, are specialist industry recruiters who can play a very important role when recruiting for senior positions.

Headhunters are almost always industry specialists. They search through their contact databases and networks to produce a list of suitable candidates for your position. These candidates may, or may not, already be employed. Often they will work in a related field in a similar organization to yours. They may even work for a leading competitor of yours. Then they approach these people direct, to discuss with them their interest and suitability for the role. If appropriate, they then pass on a shortlist to the client for further interview and assessment. Headhunters may also take part in the interview and assessment process. Sometimes they assist the client with writing the job description and person specification.

Headhunters can be expensive. Fees vary, but are usually at least one-third of the first year's guaranteed salary. This often means the complete salary, including any bonuses and extras, such as a company car. So it is unlikely that you will use a headhunter when recruiting anyone other than a senior member of staff.

Using headhunters effectively

If you plan to use a headhunter, there are several steps you can take to ensure that the recruitment process succeeds. First of all, make sure that you use the services of a headhunter with knowledge and contacts in your industry. You are paying for expertise, so you must find a suitably qualified headhunter in the first place. It may be appropriate to ask colleagues or business acquaintances in other organizations to see if you can identify recommended head-hunting firms. It is good practice to follow the same process to locate a headhunter as you would to recruit a new member of staff:

- draw up a shortlist of potential headhunters and go and meet them
- try to meet the specific contact who will be helping you
- make sure that you see examples of past work, as well as endorsements from clients and relevant references.

Each headhunting firm will have terms and conditions that define exactly what process they will undertake to find the right candidate for you. Make sure that you read these terms and conditions, and that you understand them. You should also establish exactly what the process will cost.

- What extra fees and charges are applicable other than the percentage of the successful candidate's first year's earnings?
- What happens if they fail to find a suitable candidate? Are any charges applicable?
- What if the person appointed leaves within the first six months of employment? Will the headhunter refund a percentage of the fee?

As with an agency, you must also remember to brief the head-hunting firm as thoroughly as possible. The more the headhunter understands, both about the position and the type of person you are looking for, the more likely the headhunter is to succeed in the search. Just as with using employment agencies, you should also allow plenty of opportunity for feedback. Let the headhunter know what was right and wrong about each candidate that they put forward. Ongoing feedback like this increases the chance that the headhunter will eventually find the ideal candidate.

Using headhunters can be a difficult process, but you will undoubtedly reach candidates who are otherwise unattainable. Headhunting firms will contact suitably qualified people who are already employed in other organizations. They will not wait for candidates who actively apply for roles.

Headhunters are often used:

- when the nature of the role is such that only a few people could do it
- when very few people would apply for the position
- when potential applicants are spread very thinly across an industry
- when very specific skills are required.

Disadvantages

There are a few pitfalls, however:

- Headhunters usually require quite a long period to produce the shortlist of suitable contacts. They may initially ask for around four to six weeks.
- The headhunter must have an excellent understanding of the vacancy, the organization and the type of person that you hope to recruit.
- Remember that headhunters are not always successful, so you may commit the time required for headhunting, only to end up without someone appointed to the role.
- Some time can be wasted when headhunting, because those who have been shortlisted may go through the interview and assessment process just because they are flattered to have been approached in the first place. They may have no interest in the role that you are recruiting for, or may be happy in their current position, and have no plans to leave.
- You must ensure that headhunters conduct new research, as well as just work through their existing database.

Checklist

✓ Would using an agency help with your particular recruitment needs?

✓ Would you be able to locate a suitable agency?

✓ Could you brief an agency effectively?

✓ Could you manage your relationship with an agency effectively?

✓ Can you justify the agency's costs?

✓ Will the vacancy you need to fill require the services of an expert headhunter?

✓ Can you justify a headhunter's costs?

06 other external recruitment sources

In this chapter you will learn:

- where else you might find good staff
- how to recruit graduates
- how to get the most from job fairs and open days.

Whether or not you use an agency in your hunt for the ideal candidate, there are a number of other external recruitment sources which may work for you and your organization.

Job centres

If you place details of your vacancy on a display card at the local job centre, it is likely to be seen by a large number of people, almost all of whom will be unemployed and looking for work. The staff at the job centre will encourage suitable applicants to apply for the position.

This is ideal, as long as you bear in mind one or two points. First, remember that people on benefits are often looking for *any* job, not necessarily the position you have on offer. They may turn out to be ideally suited for the position, but remember that they may not have applied initially with the same interest and passion as an applicant who has specifically applied for your job.

Second, you should bear in mind that people already in employment rarely visit job centres. So there are only certain types of job that you would advertise in a job centre alone. Often, you will need to consider other sources of recruitment as well.

You should also consider that the role of a job centre is to get people on benefits back into work as quickly as possible. So the job centre staff may encourage some less suitable candidates to apply for your vacancy. It therefore makes sense to specify to the job centre staff precisely the sort of person you are looking for.

Job centres offer their services free of charge. You can advertise your position locally, regionally or nationally. Job centre staff are able to screen applicants for you, and put forward for interview only those who seem suitable. Job centres also offer a number of additional services. For example, you can use the job centre to conduct your interviews.

Over all, the job centre can be a good source of recruitment for junior, as well as less-skilled positions. But you should rarely rely on them alone.

Job fairs

If the vacancy is not urgent, or you have several vacancies to fill, there are two types of job fair that you should consider:

1 Recruitment fairs run by commercial exhibition organizers or job centres. These take place throughout the year in regional exhibition halls and hotel conference areas. Contact your local job centre for details, or watch the regional press for forthcoming fairs in your area.

2 Careers events run by schools, colleges and universities. If you are looking for graduates, then events run by educational establishments might be the answer. They tend to attract the large organizations and public bodies, but if you are a smaller organization, and want to attend, get in touch with the careers officer at your nearest college, university or secondary school.

Job fairs are often overlooked as a good recruitment source, but they can be extremely effective. They attract a wide range of people, from the unemployed to senior managers looking for new positions. Hiring a trade stand at a job fair is expensive, so they work best when you need to fill several vacancies at once. They provide a good opportunity to meet potential candidates, and if you have time you can begin the interview process during the course of the fair.

One of the disadvantages of job fairs is that you cannot always be certain that there will be a fair at the same time that you are looking for staff. However, you may be able to predict your staffing needs such that attending one or more fairs each year is cost-effective. If yours is the sort of organization that requires a regular intake of skilled, managerial or graduate level staff, recruitment or job fairs might prove ideal.

Professional bodies, clubs and societies

Is there a professional body or organization that serves your particular industry? For example:

- Chartered Institute of Marketing (CIM)
- Institute of Management (IOM)
- Institute of Personnel and Development (IPD).

If you are a member of a relevant body or professional institute, you will probably find that there is scope to recruit from amongst their individual members or member organizations. They may publish a journal that includes a recruitment section. Or they may be happy to supply you with their mailing list. Either option is worth considering, especially as you know that any recruitment drive you undertake will be sent direct to highly targeted prospects.

Schools and colleges

If you are looking for unskilled staff for jobs that do not require previous work or related experience, you might consider contacting the local secondary schools and sixth form colleges. Most will have a dedicated careers officer with whom you can discuss your staffing requirements, and you will find that they are only too pleased to assist your recruitment campaign. There are several advantages to recruiting in this way:

- the costs of recruitment are lower
- there is often a pool of candidates to choose from
- because they have little work experience, you can mould your new recruits to your organization's culture.

However, you need to remember that most school age candidates will have had no work experience of any significance, and may be slower to adjust mentally to the working world than staff you recruit from other sources.

Talk to the careers officer about offering work placement opportunities to students. Virtually every secondary pupil will do at least a week's work experience before leaving school, and getting involved might help you to identify some workers for the future.

Open days

Open days are becoming increasingly common in larger organizations, or in companies whose profile is particularly high in the local community. The idea is to throw open the doors for a day, and encourage anyone who might be interested to take a look around, and to hear about the job and career opportunities available. You wouldn't want to host an open day for a single vacancy, but if you need to recruit for a number of positions, then it is worth considering. Open days give potential applicants the chance to:

- see your premises
- talk to you and your staff
- get a feel for what working for you might be like

- take away brochures, catalogues and other company literature.

If it is not practical to host the event on site, it might be worth holding an open session at a local hotel or conference centre. And if you hold the event in the evening or over a weekend, more candidates will be able to attend.

Internships

Internships are usually part-time roles offered to students while they are still studying at college or university. The student benefits from getting practical work experience relevant to the course they are studying. As the employer, you get the chance to employ the services of someone whom you may wish to employ full-time when they have completed their course. You can also provide the college or university with practical feedback about the relevance and value of each element of the course. Could it be improved in such a way that makes students from the course more valuable to you?

Contact your local college or university if you think an internship might work for you or your organization.

Graduate recruitment

In the past, most graduate recruitment was conducted by large organizations. These days, organizations of all types and sizes are taking advantage of the opportunity. There are a number of benefits. New or recent graduates are usually keen, intelligent, willing and untainted by years of working for other organizations.

However, graduates can be demanding. They are looking for a competitive salary and a fast track career path. If they do not think you are providing them with sufficient challenge, career progression or reward, they are likely to leave.

What are you looking for?

When recruiting graduates, you should build your person specification exactly as you would with any other recruitment method. Don't assume that because a candidate is a graduate they necessarily have the skills and attributes you are looking for. Consider the following:

- Are you looking for a subject specialist, or will a graduate of any discipline do? For example, are you looking for an engineer or computer programmer?
- What other specific skills (for example, languages) are either essential or desirable for the role?
- Are you looking for a graduate with previous work or commercial experience? Will a graduate who has undertaken a work placement qualify?

Training and development

When putting together the job description and person specification, think carefully about the future:

- What training and development opportunities exist for the graduate in the role?
- What career progression is likely/possible?
- How is the salary, and other remuneration, likely to develop in the future?

You need to put together a competitive package to attract graduates, but there is no advantage in being anything other than realistic. If the best you think you can offer is a year or so in a challenging role before the graduate will want to move on elsewhere, then it is probably best to say so.

The approach

When looking for your ideal graduate, approach two or more colleges or universities as students are often prepared to study anywhere. Don't assume that students always study at their nearest university. Talk to the careers officer, and get details of the job fairs, the milk round and the employer presentation opportunities that exist. Most universities have a system that enables employers to meet and talk to students on campus.

Agencies

If approaching the universities direct sounds like hard work, there are plenty of employment agencies around the country that have graduates on their books. They will charge a premium (up to around 25 per cent of the first year's salary), but offer a range of services, including identifying appropriate undergraduate courses, screening applicants and conducting first interviews.

Advertising

Most national newspapers have regular graduate recruitment sections. In addition, in the UK there is one national graduate weekly newspaper that is distributed around campus. It is called *Prospects Today*. Their website is at www.prospects.csu.ac.uk.

Finally, remember that if you plan to take on a graduate, you must keep them motivated and challenged in their role. They will expect the best training and development you can offer, as well as periodic salary and career reviews.

Checklist

✓ Could a job centre help in your search for the ideal recruit?
✓ Are there any job fairs you can attend, either locally or nationally?
✓ Are you a member of a professional body, club or society that can help you to recruit your new staff member?
✓ Is it worth contacting local secondary schools and sixth form colleges for this, or other vacancies?
✓ How about hosting an open day at your company or organization?
✓ Could you offer an internship to a part-qualified student?
✓ Does your vacancy demand a graduate?

07

online recruitment

In this chapter you will learn:

- which are the best recruitment sites
- how to make your own website work for you
- how to write an online job advertisement.

> Increasingly organizations are using the internet as a recruitment source. There are hundreds of recruitment sites online, so where do you begin? How can you be sure that your vacancy will be seen by suitable candidates?

What is online recruitment?

At its most simple, online recruitment involves placing details of your job vacancies on a website. It could be your organization's own website, or a third party site that is dedicated wholly to the business of recruitment. But recruiting online can be a lot more sophisticated than that.

Specialist online recruitment sites almost always permit electronic submissions, meaning that potential applicants can read the job description and person specification, complete an application form and submit a CV, all online, and entirely electronically. There is no need for the candidate to request an application form, and all the applications will arrive, in identical format, in your inbox along with the rest of your e-mail. Some sites will even search applications for particular keywords entered, and give them higher priority. For example, if there is a particular skill that you consider essential, and an applicant lists this skill in his or her electronic application, it will be given a higher priority than someone who has not listed the skill.

Internet growth

The Chartered Institute of Personnel and Development (CIPD) publishes regular surveys that indicate a dramatic increase in the number of companies making use of the internet for recruitment purposes. According to a CIPD survey in November 2002:

- 75 per cent of recruiters were using e-mail to handle job applications or enquiries.
- More than 50 per cent used their company website to advertise jobs.
- Over 22 per cent of employers accepted completed applications by e-mail.
- 98 per cent of graduates have internet access at college or university, and the majority of these will spend time online looking at career options in their final year.

- So far, less than 1 per cent of organizations are administering selection tests online.

However, the survey concluded that there is little evidence to suggest that recruiters are using electronic tools to do anything more than widen their exposure to potential applicants. In other words, the internet is not yet replacing traditional recruiting methods. Rather, it is establishing itself as one of a number of recruitment tools that, used together, make up a successful recruitment process.

Where online?

Typically there are three types of internet site where you might want to advertise your vacancies:

1. Your own company website. As the CIPD survey indicates, more than 50 per cent of employers post details of their vacancies on their own organization's website. It is a quick and reasonably inexpensive process, although unless your organization is particularly well known, it may not be very effective. After all, how would an applicant know to look on your website? Job hunters tend to go first to websites listing vacancies from a number of companies and organizations. However, if you advertise the position in the press, it is useful to be able to send applicants to the website for further details about the job, as well as a job description and person specification that they can download.

2. Dedicated recruitment sites. There are literally thousands of websites dedicated to the recruitment and selection of staff. It can be hard to know which recruitment website is likely to be suitable for your needs. Nevertheless, at the end of the chapter we have listed a number of the larger and longer established recruitment websites that are recommended for general and lower-skilled vacancies. For specialist positions, there are a number of websites, newsgroups, forums and bulletin boards where job seekers in certain industries are likely to look for work. For example, there are websites that specialize in advertising vacancies relating to personnel, and training and development. It is worth saying that workers in more technical industries, such as computer programmers, are more accustomed to using the internet for recruitment than other workers.

3 Media sites. Increasingly, if you advertise a vacancy with a national newspaper, details of the vacancy will also appear on the newspaper's website. This can make advertising in newspapers good value, as you are increasing your exposure to potential applicants. Indeed, many job seekers prefer the web interface, because it allows them to narrow down their search for specific job types by keywords.

Advantages and disadvantages

Just as with any other recruitment method, there are advantages and disadvantages associated with internet recruitment.

Advantages

- The internet can reduce the time it takes to recruit new staff.
- With care, it can reduce many of the costs, particularly administrative, associated with recruitment.
- The internet gives you access to a broader pool of potential applicants.
- It enables you to advertise your positions across continents, if appropriate.
- Using the internet for recruitment suggests to applicants that yours is a modern, forward-looking organization.
- It is arguably the best way to reach applicants from certain sectors, such as Computing and Information Technology.

Disadvantages

- Most job hunters will look at websites as well as, but not instead of, traditional recruitment media. So it is not yet the first choice recruitment source.
- Not everyone has access to the internet (or, more commonly, they have internet access at their current employment, where it would be inappropriate to be seen visiting recruitment websites).
- Online applications make applying for a job much easier and less of an effort, and so you may receive a greater proportion of applications from unsuitable candidates.
- Until internet access is universal, online recruitment will usually be undertaken alongside traditional recruitment methods, and so add to costs, rather than reduce them.

Using online and offline together

There is little point in going to the trouble of using the internet as part of the recruitment process, if all you plan to do is repeat the information that you have already laid out in the press, or posted on to your staff notice board. The internet works best when it enhances what else you do. Consider the model below:

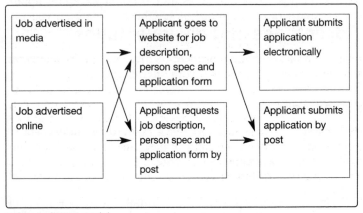

web recruitment model

In this model, you would include a web address in your press advertisement, where potential applicants can go for further details of the position (as well as a telephone number for applicants without internet access).

If you do not feel comfortable with the idea of electronic applications, you could include an application form online that should be printed out and completed by hand. Or perhaps you should encourage applicants to e-mail your organization to request a paper application form. The idea is to use the internet to improve the recruitment process, not to make it more complicated.

Taking it one stage further

There are more ways to use online recruitment websites other than simply to advertise jobs. When looking for work, job hunters will often post their CV, and register their job interests, on one or more recruitment websites. This is good news for employers. For a small fee, you can search a database of job hunters by keywords. You can then review a shortlist of candidates that match your search criteria, without having actually advertised your vacancy online. In addition, you may have to pay the online agency a percentage of the successful candidate's salary, just as with traditional recruitment agencies.

Other more sophisticated services are available when recruiting for staff online. For example, a number of specialist organizations have developed software that reviews incoming electronic applications, and screens and shortlists suitable candidates. If yours is a larger organization that tends to receive hundreds of applications for dozens of positions on a regular basis, you might want to investigate this software more thoroughly. Most of the screening software applications work by searching electronic applications for particular phrases or keywords which, if present, indicate certain qualifications or experience that the candidate has. Clever, but not infallible. For example, the candidate may have made sure that his application included all of the essential and desirable criteria listed in the advertisement. It also assumes that you can define the list of keywords that you want to search applications for. What about all the other selection criteria, such as personality?

Using screening software is good for filtering out candidates who are clearly unqualified for the role, but may not be as effective for shortlisting ideally suited candidates. Nevertheless, technology is progressing all the time, so it is worth checking out what software is available for assisting with online recruitment when you are ready to recruit.

The future

Inevitably, we can look to the USA for an indication about where online recruitment technology is progressing. How about online interviews? Would you ever take on a member of staff without having ever met them face to face, even for a few minutes? Some companies in the USA are already conducting online interviews for low-skilled, general positions. Online assessments, like psychometric or aptitude tests, are already being used in the UK, as the following article in *People Management*, from February 2003, clearly illustrates:

You can do it . . .

Online recruitment using psychometrics has been so successful at managerial level that B&Q has decided to extend the process to the shopfloor.

Faced with an increasingly tight retail-management recruitment market, DIY giant B&Q has enlisted the help of psychology to radically alter its hiring strategy. The company introduced online psychometric testing for all managerial candidates in July, and intends to extend the scheme to all shopfloor staff this month.

According to B&Q, the system is already reaping benefits. 'It cost £120,000 to build the system and develop the psychometric test, which we will recoup within a year,' says Rob Barnett, policy and services controller. 'It has saved us 60 per cent in terms of time and 30 per cent in costs, so it has made a compelling case for extending it. But the biggest reason for doing it initially was to improve the quality of our managers.'

Applicants answer a range of questions and their answers are assessed immediately – by complex formulae – to predict whether they have the appropriate personality for the job. The idea is that, by quickly eliminating unsuitable candidates, the initial stage of recruitment is streamlined and a database of potential recruits built up.

Candidates also receive immediate feedback on their suitability, while the rest of the hiring process is conducted in the traditional manner, through interviews at the stores.

The psychometric test, open to anyone who accesses B&Q's site (http://www.diy.com/), is not bespoke, but was developed over the course of seven years by Colin Gill, chief psychologist at Psychological Solutions. Much of the research was conducted on B&Q staff, and the company is the first to use it.

Gill says, 'We assess candidates' personalities and the results go through a series of mathematical calculations to assess their job performance. The problem with most existing questionnaires is that they are statement-based, for example: "Do you like meeting people at parties?" The answer tends to depend on the last party they went to. Our questionnaire, on the other hand, only uses adjectives in a clear occupational reference and so cuts out a lot of possible misinterpretations, we would say for example: "Are you outgoing?"

Gill claims the test was designed to take into account that candidates' perceptions of themselves might drastically differ from reality. B&Q introduced the system because, as retail managers are at a premium, competition for talent is fierce within the sector. A third of all the 15,000 jobs available at the company each year are new positions created by the opening of new stores. So the need for managers far outstripped the amount that could be promoted internally.

'We create about 1,000 new management jobs each year, and are perpetually hungry for new staff,' says HR director Mike Cutt. B&Q has supercentres that employ 40–50 staff, and warehouse stores with about 250 staff.

He says the new system also gives the recruitment process a built-in mechanism to counteract inherent prejudice, during the initial stages of recruitment at least.

'Our image of candidates used to be founded on their CVs. Now the initial screening is done blind, it is totally unbiased as to age, gender and ethnic background. We think that's a big step forward in systematically avoiding the bias you would get in any recruitment drive.'

But has the system achieved its objective of improving quality? Cutt is emphatic that it has. 'The quality of our candidates is certainly going up,' he says.

'We have what we call our "triple A" candidates, who match our requirements exactly, so this system doesn't just screen people "in" or "out", but tells us who the "triple A" people are and allows us to see their full potential. It means we can spot potential talent earlier, and allows recruitment and development to become more closely aligned.'

There was some scepticism when Cutt first approached his board with the idea. 'Cynics often say that psychometrics is a load of rubbish, and sometimes there's resistance to taking some control out of the hands of line managers,' he says.

'It does decentralise recruitment, so it is disempowering for line managers who might want to retain ownership of that process. But although you are taking some of their work away from them, they still make the final interviewing and hiring decision.'

(source: *People Management*, 20 February, 2003. Author: Elizabeth Davidson)

Which are the best agencies?

There are too many online agencies to make a sensible list in this book. In any case, new agencies are appearing online every week, whilst others struggle to survive. We have listed below three agencies that have seen dramatic growth over of the last two years, and which attract candidates from a wide spectrum of careers.

www.monster.co.uk

At Monster, you can post details of a job at any time, day or night. Prices currently start at £250 for 60 days. Additional services include help with writing advertisements, Applicant Tracking Solutions, and even complete outsourcing of the recruitment process. As with many other recruitment websites, you can search Monster's CV database directly, without waiting for candidates to see your advertisement. At the time of writing, Monster has over 500,000 job hunters registered.

www.fish4jobs.co.uk

fish4jobs claims to be the UK's No. 1 recruitment website. You can post details of your vacancy on their website for £275 for four weeks. The price includes a page where you can detail a full company profile, giving further details about your organization. Fish4jobs has close associations with hundreds of local newspapers, and offers a service whereby you can advertise both on the website and in the local newspaper of your choice.

www.workthing.com

Like the other sites, www.workthing.com offers database searching, help with writing advertisements and a range of job posting options. In addition, Workthing offers a suite of tools enabling you to sift your job applications for keywords and phrases to shortlist candidates quickly. You can then use their bulk e-mailing feature to contact all candidates easily. Prices for the standard job posting service are comparable with the websites listed above.

If you think that an online recruitment campaign might help or support your search for the right applicant, then do a bit of research before you start. There are specialist online recruitment companies serving certain industries, and there are hundreds of other general agencies that offer similar services to the websites that we have featured.

Writing an online job advertisement

Although we provide a short guide to writing effective recruitment advertisements elsewhere in this book, there are some special rules you should follow when composing advertisements for recruitment websites.

Make it stand out

In print, you make your advertisement stand out with colour, design, size and position. Online, it is highly unlikely that job hunters will 'browse' in the traditional way. They are far more likely to search for jobs by keywords. So to make sure your advertisement is seen by the widest possible audience, think of all the words or phrases that best describe the vacancy, and which job hunters might enter into a database. Construct the wording of your advertisement around these words and phrases.

What should be included

Online job hunters will be looking at a summary list of appropriate vacancies, and will make a snap decision about which jobs to find out more about and apply for. Unlike traditional recruitment advertisements, there are a number of elements that you should include online, like salary, the company name and location, as well as any benefits or bonuses. You also want to restrict unqualified people from applying, so state clearly any qualification or minimum experience requirements.

On the whole, you are better off giving more details about the position you are trying to fill than you would in a print environment. You will find that there is plenty of help and advice available online when you post details of a job vacancy, and most online recruitment organizations offer help with the wording of any advertisement that you place. Spend some time looking at the way other recruitment advertisements are written online, before writing your own.

Checklist

✓ Have you posted details of your vacancies on your organization's intranet or website?
✓ Have you considered using a dedicated online recruitment website?
✓ Are your press recruitment advertisements replicated on the newspaper's or journal's website?
✓ Have you researched which web agencies would best suit your needs?
✓ Could you write an online recruitment advertisement?

08
advertising positions

In this chapter you will learn:

- how to write a recruitment advertisement
- how to make your advertisement stand out
- how to get value for money
- how to measure the effectiveness of your advertisement.

Whether you are recruiting internally or externally, at some stage you will need to put together an advertisement that describes the position and invites applications. But how should you word one? What should you include?

Writing a recruitment advertisement

Anyone will tell you that the purpose of a recruitment advertisement is to attract good candidates. Just as important, however, is an advertisement's ability to discourage unsuitable applicants from applying. You want to avoid having to sift through hundreds of applications, trying to identify the few genuine, suitable ones.

Every recruitment advertisement you place will be different. A card placed in the newsagent's window will say something different from a poster in your local job centre. The wording used in a trade journal advertisement will be different from that in a national Sunday newspaper. So you should avoid adopting the same approach each time you need to advertise. Nevertheless, there are general principles that you should follow regardless of where you intend to advertise.

Company details

Unless you particularly want to hide the fact that you are recruiting, it is important to state clearly the organization's name and details. If your organization is well known, locally or nationally, your name and logo will immediately stand out in a crowded jobs page, and this is what you want to achieve. Moreover, research has shown that candidates want to know who they are applying to work for.

Some companies choose to imply, rather than state, their name. This is okay, but think carefully before adopting this approach. If your advertisement states 'leading drinks manufacturer', many applicants will assume that the position is with Coca-Cola, and will be disappointed if this turns out not to be the case.

The company name should not be the most prominent feature of the advertisement, however well known it is. You are recruiting for a specific position, and you want to ensure that only the qualified apply. So the position itself should stand out above all else.

Job title

This is the most important detail to get across in a recruitment advertisement. Make this prominent, and it ought to attract the attention only of those qualified to do it. In other words, you will immediately filter out a number of candidates who are applying for jobs for which they are not qualified.

You must ensure that the job title is specific and realistic. There is no need to dress up a job to make it sound more interesting or important than it is. For example:

Telephone Sales	rather than	Field Marketing Executive
Complaints Handler	rather than	Quality Adviser

Applicants should be under no illusion about what they are applying for. If you say it how it is, you can be sure that applicants are applying for broadly the right reasons.

Location

Although not essential, stating the location of the job provides another means of filtering unsuitable candidates. Some people either do not want to, or are not able to, work where the position is based. Better that they do not apply, rather than find out after you have wasted time interviewing them.

Salary

Stating salary can be tricky. You may not want your competitors or your staff knowing what you pay. But stating salary is another means of filtering, and can reduce significantly the number of unsuitable applications that you receive.

If you are unsure about salary, at least put in an upper and lower band, even if this is quite wide. Many companies make broad statements like:

* excellent remuneration package
* first class salary.

Be wary of making such statements. For a position paying £25,000, some applicants would regard £12,500 as excellent remuneration, while others would assume that the position probably pays £40,000. You would not want to employ the former category, and you are unlikely to be able to agree terms with the latter. If you state the salary band that you are offering, you ensure that you receive applications from candidates with realistic salary expectations.

Job requirements

The space that you can devote to the requirements of the job depends on the size of the advertisement that you have placed. However, you should think carefully about the most important job requirements, and make sure that these are stated clearly. Use the job specification you prepared earlier to help you with this. List the main job requirements as bullet points to save space, and make clear where specific experience or expertise is required. Highlight the interesting and exciting aspects of the job, by all means, but make sure that you cover the dull bits as well. You want to be transparent about what the role involves.

State the responsibilities and seniority of the role. This will give candidates a feel for the level of job that they are applying for, and the experience that they are likely to need. Unqualified candidates may choose not to apply, saving you valuable time at the shortlisting stages.

Person requirements

This is your opportunity to describe, as closely as you can, the type of person you are looking for. What qualifications must they have? What experience is essential? One often sees advertisements that list both the essential and the desirable experience and qualifications sought. This is an effective means of ensuring that only candidates with the right experience will apply. You should be able to list the main person requirements from the person specification that you have already prepared.

Prospects

If the position you are trying to fill has genuine prospects, then you should say so. But do not exaggerate. You do not want to recruit someone who becomes dissatisfied because they are not progressing up through the organization quickly enough.

Be realistic. If it is a low level job requiring few skills, then emphasize the stability of the role, rather than its prospects. An ambitious person appointed to a mundane role will soon become restless.

How to apply

You should give clear instructions about how candidates should apply for the position. Should candidates submit a CV with covering letter? Should they request an application form by telephone first? State clearly who and where they should apply to. If you are worried about applications going astray, ask candidates to mark their envelopes with a reference number so that they can be identified when the mail is delivered, and dealt with separately.

It is also a good idea to state a closing date for applications. There are two reasons for this. First, you want interested candidates to get on with submitting their applications. Second, some newspapers post job advertisements automatically onto online recruitment sites, and these can appear several weeks after you originally placed the advertisement. By stating a closing date, you ensure that you do not waste applicants' time applying for vacancies that have already been filled.

Checklist

Use the following checklist to make sure that you include the key elements of your advertisement.

Job title
Location
Company name and details
Job requirements (tasks and responsibilities)
Person requirements (experience and qualifications)
    Essential
    Desirable
Salary
Prospects
How to apply
Closing date for applications

Making your advertisement stand out

If you are placing your advertisement in a newspaper or trade journal, the chances are that yours will be just one out of several hundred others on the same pages. How can you make sure that your advertisement stands the best chance of being read and acted on?

Your advertisement must drive prospective candidates through four distinct stages:

Attention

You want the advertisement to attract the attention of those with the right qualifications and experience for the role.

↓

Interest

You want to create interest in the vacancy.

↓

Desire

You want those with the right experience to think 'This is the job for me! I want this job!'

↓

Action

You want those people to apply for the position straight away.

It is a lot to expect of a small advertisement that it will drive the right candidates through each of these four stages. We have already considered how the wording and contents of the advertisement can ensure that the right people apply. But there is a lot that you can do to increase the chances of the advertisement being noticed in the first place. Here are some examples:

Position

Try to negotiate a strong position for the advertisement within the newspaper or journal when you place the booking. Is there room on the first page of jobs? The last page? The front or back cover? It often costs extra, but if it means that more people see your advertisement, then it will be worth the additional investment.

Size

Clearly, the bigger the advertisement, the more likely it is to be seen. However, do not feel pressured into buying more advertising space. There are plenty of other ways to make your vacancy stand out from the others.

Colour

A colour advertisement will often stand out, especially if the majority of other vacancies are in black and white. Again, colour advertisements will add to the cost considerably, and it may be more effective to book a larger black and white space, rather than a smaller, colour one.

Design

Sensible, eye-catching design features add nothing to the cost of placing the advertisement, but add considerably to its impact. Choose a thick border, and use bold headings for the job title or company name. Using an unusual shape, or just a different shape to everyone else, ensures that it will stand out. Be creative with typefaces and fonts. How about a light shading? There is no need to go mad. You just need to make sure that your advertisement is that bit more prominent than anyone else's.

Your organization's logo will probably make the advertisement more eye catching, particularly if it is distinctive and well known, locally or nationally. You may be restricted in the way that you use the logo and typeface, especially if your organization has a house style with which all printed publicity must comply.

Just because you have paid for the space, there is no need to fill it. Too many words, and you will put people off. The advertisement's role is to generate interest, not to give every detail about the vacancy. So leave plenty of white space, and be brief.

Copy

Avoid jargon or technical terms that only others in your industry will understand. It tends not to impress, and may discourage otherwise good candidates from applying. Humour is another element to consider very carefully. Humour is subjective and personal, and what is funny to one person might be taken seriously by another. If you work in a friendly and casual environment, you may feel you want this to come across in your advertisement. Resist the temptation, as you will have plenty of opportunity to get across your organization's work ethic and style at interview.

Overall, if you are in any doubt about whether a phrase or sentence is necessary, leave it out.

Tip

If you are writing an advertisement that will be placed on a website, there are specific rules you should follow. Refer to Chapter 7, on Online Recruitment, for further details.

Discrimination

Before you submit your advertisement, check it thoroughly for any signs of discrimination. It is illegal to specify the preferred age, race or gender of the person you are looking for in any circumstances. Check your wording for unintentional discrimination, such as:

Salesman	rather than	Salesperson
Barmaid	rather than	Barperson
He or She	rather than	He/She or The applicant

Consider avoiding any accusation of discrimination by stating clearly your organization's policy on the subject:

We welcome applications from qualified people regardless of race, gender, age or disability. We are an equal opportunities employer.

You should also review the appendix on discrimination, starting on page 199.

It would be impossible to design a template for a job advertisement that would work in all situations, for all vacancies. The examples starting on page 80 do, however, illustrate how to bring the wording and design together to make the overall effect eye catching and interesting to read (to the right person!).

Checklist

Use the following checklist when designing your job advertisement, to make sure that it has maximum impact.

Does the advertisement grab attention?	(✓)
• position	
• size	
• colour	
• shape	
• border	
• typeface	
• logo	
Is it interesting?	
• brief and concise	
• plenty of white space	

Are you putting applicants off?
- discrimination
- jargon
- humour

Is there a call to action?
- closing date

How to apply

Central College of Management

CCM

Part-time Distance Learning Tutors
MSc in Performance Management
MSc in Economics
Postgraduate Diploma in Management

CCM is a distance learning organization and teaches Masters and Postgraduate Diploma students in subjects such as finance economics and management.

We are looking to recruit additional tutors for the programmes listed above. The successful applicant will provide feedback to students, mark assignments and assist in programme development if appropriate.

For more information, an application form and a job description, please contact: The Personnel Department, Central College of Management, Queens Road, Cambridge.
CVs will only be accepted if accompanied by an application form. Closing date: 15 February 2004.

sample job advertisement

Recruitment Direct ≣*RD*≣

Assistant Employment Officers
Competitive starting salary and a generous
benefits package
Based in the South East

Thousands of people are looking for a new job at any one time, whether they are school leavers, graduates, or those seeking promotion or a change in direction.

And that's where you come in. As an Assistant Employment Officer, you will support the work of Recruitment Direct by carrying out a range of interesting tasks: gathering information on both the target company and the candidate; liaising with companies to find out what they need; working with candidates on their presentation; and interviewing candidates.

It will be a challenge and you will need to be a fast thinker and learner. An open mind and an ability to communicate is critical. You will be required to prove that you have the relevant qualifications and appropriate experience.

For an application, call 0845 9999 222. Please quote reference 551551. Closing date for receipt of completed applications 31 March 2004.

Recruitment Direct is an equal opportunities employer.

sample job advertisement

Fruit and Veg Mart
Quality Control Testers

We are looking for Quality Control Testers to work in our produce distribution centre. The job involves checking and recording the quality of a variety of fresh produce. Successful candidates will show a sound knowledge of produce. You will demonstrate a keen eye for detail and be able to work under pressure. You will work six days in eight, on a continuous shift rotation and receive an excellent remuneration package.

Please send your CV and covering letter to: Jayesh Patel, Quality Control Manager, Fruit and Veg Mart, 118 Bridge Road, Coventry.

sample job advertisement

Media choice

The response that you get to your recruitment advertisement depends not just upon how it is worded, but also where you choose to advertise. Your choice of media will influence both the type and number of applicants that you receive. There is a wide choice available to you.

Trade publications

If the position you are trying to fill demands specialist skills, then a trade journal or newsletter might prove to be the ideal choice. These tend to be read mainly by those in the industry, or by people who are looking to work in the industry. So you can be pretty certain that suitably qualified people will read your advertisement.

Local press

Local newspapers often have a regular recruitment section covering a wide local area. Although they usually cover jobs from a wide range of sectors, they are often the first place that a job seeker will look in their search for work. Local newspapers are particularly suitable for low skilled or junior positions. If the mix of skills you are looking for is common, you can advertise in the local press confident that you will attract a reasonable number of applicants. Since advertising locally is almost always cheaper than advertising in the national press, you will save money as well. However, if the mix of skills you are looking for is rare, you may have to advertise in the national press in order to locate a sufficient number of candidates.

National press

To broaden your search, you should consider placing your advertisement in the recruitment section of one of the national daily newspapers. Many broadsheet newspapers devote dedicated recruitment space to specific industries on different days. For example, the *Guardian* specializes in marketing and media jobs on a Monday. So most people in the marketing sector know that if they are looking for a new job, they should read the *Guardian* on a Monday.

Billboards

It is not always necessary to use the press. Your organization may have a public notice board or billboard, for example, near the entrance gates. If the public regularly walk past your offices, you may find that placing your advertisement in a prominent position on a billboard will attract a sufficient number of applicants. Again the level of success depends on the type of position that you are trying to fill. It is unlikely that you will recruit a new chief executive through an advertisement placed on a billboard, but you may recruit junior factory workers, administrative and other staff in this way.

If you do not have a billboard, why not try placing the advertisement in a shop window? If yours is a retail business, you may find new staff from amongst your existing customers. So placing an advertisement in your shop window may attract the ideal candidate. Alternatively, place your advertisement in the window of another outlet, like the local newsagent's or post office.

Radio

Using the radio for recruitment is becoming increasingly popular, although it can be expensive. You also have to plan the timing of the broadcasts carefully, as you are reliant on the captive audience at the time. Recruitment advertisements are usually broadcast when people are getting up in the morning, travelling to work, having their lunch, returning home, and so on.

You will need professional help if you plan to recruit staff using the radio. The wording of your message has to be carefully scripted and planned. It will need to be catchy and memorable. You also need to ensure that any call to action, like phoning a number for an application form, is simple. You may even have to obtain a telephone number that is easy to remember.

Readership and circulation

When selecting the media that you use, there is a lot of useful research that you can do. For example, you should find out the circulation and readership figures for any journal or newspaper that you plan to use. The 'circulation' figures indicate how many copies of each issue of the newspaper are sold or distributed. The 'readership' will give you an idea about the type of people who read it. Newspapers and journals will often claim that their readership figure is much higher than their circulation figure. This is because each issue of a journal purchased by an office, for example, will be distributed amongst several staff before it is thrown away. You should take particular note of the readership statistics, as they may throw light on how suitable the journal or newspaper is for your particular recruitment requirements. An annual National Readership Survey, published by the media owners, gives figures based on the main professions, showing, for example, how many accountants read each national newspaper.

Negotiating rates and position

In the recruitment media, sales people expect to have to negotiate or haggle over the rates that they charge. As a result, they usually publish a rate card, listing charges for advertising space of different sizes and positions. Ask to see the rate card for the newspaper or journal that you have decided to advertise in. Treat the prices quoted as the absolute maximum that you should pay. You ought to be able to negotiate a healthy discount from the rate card, with the discount increasing for placing more, or larger, advertisements.

Measuring an advertisement's effectiveness

Some advertisements work, and others do not. It is very important that you evaluate, as far as possible, how effective each advertisement that you place is. You should record:

- when the advertisement appeared
- which newspaper/journal
- the exact position within the pages of the newspaper/journal
- the cost of the advertisement
- the number of applicants
- approximate percentage of suitably qualified applicants
- number of candidates shortlisted
- candidate appointed: Yes/No

If you record each of the details listed above, you can work out very simply how cost-effective the advertisement was.

Checklist

✓ Have you included all the relevant details in your advertisement?

✓ Does your advertisement stand out?

✓ Does it grab your attention?

✓ Where will you place the advertisement?

✓ Have you made sure that your advertisement does not discriminate in any way?

✓ Have you negotiated the best rate you can?

✓ Have you negotiated a suitable position for your advertisement in the journal or newspaper?

✓ Have you put in place measures that will enable you to measure the effectiveness of the advertisement?

09

application forms

In this chapter you will learn:

- when it is appropriate to use an application form
- what application forms can tell you about a candidate
- how to design an application form.

Whether you plan to recruit online or offline, by yourself or with help from an agency, you need to consider how applicants will submit their applications. Traditionally, you would ask candidates to submit a CV with covering letter. Whilst this may still work for you, increasingly organizations are adopting dedicated application forms, which request specific information from each applicant. So, would an application form work best for you? How would you go about making one?

Increasingly, organizations request that job seekers complete a dedicated application form, rather than simply send in a CV with covering letter. An application form allows for the information needed by the employer to be presented in a consistent and uniform manner, and simplifies the job of comparing two separate applications. Using an application form ensures that applicants supply all the facts required, and that any skills gaps or career breaks are obvious. The job of shortlisting applicants for interview is made easier, as information about each applicant is presented in the same place in each application.

Questions to ask

Your organization may have standard job application forms that are used for all vacancies, regardless of the requirements or seniority of the role. Alternatively, you might be creating an application form for the first time to use for a single vacancy. In either event, you will want to collect information in a number of key areas:

- full name
- home address and telephone number
- name of employer and work telephone number
- age/date of birth
- employment history
- education
- training
- hobbies and interests
- references.

In addition, you will probably want to get candidates thinking about their reasons for applying for the vacancy, perhaps by asking questions such as:

Q Please use this section to tell us how you feel you meet the requirements of the enclosed Person Specification. Give as much information as necessary to demonstrate the skills, experience and knowledge you have gained. This could include voluntary work, leisure interests and any other activities that you consider relevant to this position.

Q Use this section to say why you want this job, how you believe that you are suited to it and what you feel you can contribute to this organization.

Many organizations use data supplied from application forms for statistical monitoring of their equal opportunities policy. Questions on the form regarding sex, race or gender are asked on a separate removable sheet, and are not used as part of the interview selection process. Over a fixed period, an organization can compare the race and gender mix of job applicants with the mix of those appointed to the positions.

You will find an example of a complete job application form, with sample questions, opposite.

Advantages of using application forms

The benefit of using applications forms comes when you start receiving applications through the post. It is much easier to compare individual applicants who have supplied answers to exactly the same list of questions, and have displayed their answers in the same place on each form. Applicants will need to supply succinct answers to your questions because space on the application form is limited. So they will not be able to waffle, and they will have to think very carefully about the experience that they consider most relevant to the vacancy on offer.

There are other advantages to using application forms. When assessing CVs, it is easy to get carried away by a particular qualification or experience that a candidate has, even though it is not a fundamental requirement of the position. By using an application form you are considering only the skills and experience that you consider relevant to the position you wish to fill.

Application forms can also help an organization's discrimination and fairness policy. All applicants begin the application process on a level footing, and all personal details regarding sex, race and gender are recorded at the front or back of the application form. So it is straightforward for you to monitor the racial mix of the applications you receive, leaving you less vulnerable to challenges of unfairness or discrimination.

Some organizations record the details of all applicants onto a database and are then able to acknowledge applications, invite candidates to interview and reject unsuccessful candidates, all using a simple mail merge operation. As long as you abide by all the requirements of the latest data protection legislation, you can also use the database to search for suitable candidates for future job vacancies. It is much easier to extract data from an application form, than from a CV and covering letter.

Disadvantages of using application forms

The use of job application forms can reduce significantly the number of applications that you receive. From a candidate's point of view, applying for a job using an application form is a lengthy and time-consuming operation. It is harder for an applicant to avoid addressing areas of weakness, and they may decide not to apply at all. Whilst this means that the applications that you do receive ought to be serious ones, you may miss out on applicants who satisfy most, but not all, of your criteria. There is no doubt that application forms are more suited to certain jobs than to others. If you are trying to fill an administrative position, with a number of essential person requirements, then the use of an application form is ideal. For more senior or management positions, you may decide that a CV with covering letter is more appropriate.

The other disadvantage of application forms is the cost, both in time and money, of designing, printing and distributing the forms to applicants. A job advertisement will often quote a telephone number for applicants to register for an application form, and this extra process will need to be administered. Although many job application forms are now available to download from an organization's website, you will still need to offer an alternative for those without internet access.

Designing a job application form

Designing a job application form is a time-consuming process, and requires a good deal of planning. You have only a limited amount of space to request all the relevant information needed to

Application for Employment

Please complete in black type.

Post for which you are applying: Ref: Number:

Completed forms to be returned to:

Family Name:

Title: Mr If other:

First Name(s):

Date of Birth: /   /

Home Telephone No: Mobile Phone Number:

Home Address

Post Code

Current or most recent employment
Job Title:
Start Date: /   /
Leaving Date or Notice Required:
Current Salary: Grade:
Employer's Name and Address:

Work Telephone No:
Duties and Responsibilities:

sample application form

Employment history

Please start with the most recent after that shown under current or most recent employment on page 1.

Starting Date: Leaving Date:

Employer's Name:

Address:

Position Held: Salary on Leaving:

Duties and responsibilities:

Reason for Leaving:

Education

Please state qualifications gained for which you will need to provide evidence

Schools, Colleges, Universities or Institute of Further Education attended (including part-time)	Dates From	To	Qualifications gained including subjects, grades or results expected

Any relevant qualifications or records of achievement (e.g. courses attended), including membership and status of any relevant Professional or Technical Association

General experience and further information

(Please photocopy and attach and number additional sheets, as necessary)

Please use this section to tell us how you feel you meet the requirements of the Person Specification. Give as much information as necessary to demonstrate the skills, experience and knowledge you have gained. This could include voluntary work, leisure interests and any other activities which you consider relevant to this position.

sample application form continued

make an informed shortlist of candidates to interview. So spend some time thinking about what you need to know, and how much space would be required to do justice to the questions you are asking. It is common practice to allow candidates to add follow-on sheets where necessary, but you should ensure that you provide sufficient space on the form for most applicants to complete their answers. You also need to consider *how* candidates will complete the application form. Will they complete them by hand? If so, you need to leave sufficient space to allow someone with larger than average handwriting to supply an adequate answer. On the other hand, many applicants will word process their application, and so less space for each answer will be required.

It is important that the application form is not too long, otherwise you will put off a number of potentially good candidates from applying. Four sides of A4 is ideal, six sides is okay, and eight sides is too many. The sample application form on pages 90 and 91 shows how you can request a lot of information in a relatively restricted space.

Consider also the different ways that the application form might be used. Will you allow candidates to complete an application form online? If so, you might want to list the questions to be completed, and provide a word limit for each one. For example:

Give brief details of current employment (max. 250 words)

What application forms can reveal

Because application forms spell out the specific information required by shortlisters, they can often reveal information about a candidate that might otherwise be hidden in a CV or covering letter: career breaks and gaps; skills shortages; absence of specific work experience; missing qualifications; weaknesses in the applicant's career relevance.

Checklist

✓ Are application forms appropriate for the vacancy you are trying to fill?
✓ Will you make the application form available online as well as offline?
✓ Have you thought about what questions to ask?
✓ Could you design your own application form, or do you know someone who could help you to design one?

part

three

assessing applications

dealing with the response

In this chapter you will learn:

- how to shortlist candidates
- how to deal with a large or small response
- about acknowledging applications
- how to reject unsuitable candidates.

If you have advertised your vacancy effectively, then you should receive a suitable number of applications on or before the set closing date. Your role now is to decide which applicants to invite for interview, and which to reject.

The response you get to a recruitment advertisement will vary dramatically according to these, and many more factors:

- nature of role
- seniority of role
- perceived popularity of job
- the organization
- the salary and benefits offered
- time of year.

In simple terms, you are likely to receive a bigger response if you are recruiting for a sales assistant than if you are looking for a nuclear physicist. However, whatever the size of response that you get, you will still need to identify which applications are worth considering and which are not. So your first job is to reduce the number of applications that you have received to a manageable size for interview.

The optimum number of candidates to interview depends on a number of factors:

- the number of vacancies you are trying to fill
- the nature and size of the organization you work for
- the number of colleagues involved in the interview process
- the urgency of the vacancy.

For a small organization looking to appoint a new salesperson, shortlisting 6–8 candidates for interview is probably about right. For a large organization recruiting 25 new call centre staff, interviewing 100 candidates might not be enough. How many is right for you? If you plan to conduct the interviews alone, you really must aim to reduce the list to a maximum of 10 candidates.

You may already have a feel for the number of candidates that you plan to interview. So your job now is to compile a suitable and fair shortlist.

How to shortlist?

Certain experienced shortlisters will read every application in full before beginning to shortlist. There is a good argument for this, and we will look at several methods that organizations adopt to make the shortlisting process simple and effective. However, if you have only received a few applications, this quick three-step shortlisting method may work for you:

Step 1: Reject obviously unsuitable candidates

This can be controversial. Usually, you will receive a few applications that are clearly unsuitable. If you have requested a hand-written application, and someone has applied in type, then there is a case for rejecting them without further consideration. After all, it may be a vacancy for which attention to detail is important, and they have clearly failed to follow a simple instruction. You may also have received one or two 'gimmicky' applications. These should also be rejected. We discuss how to identify these a little later.

Step 2: Review the person specification

Compare each application with the person specification that you created at the start of the recruitment process. You can legitimately reject those candidates who do not meet all of the essential requirements specified.

Step 3: Inclusion

The first two steps are a little negative. You are rejecting candidates who are not suitable for the position. You may find that the pile of applications remaining is sufficiently small to interview them all. If you still have a sizeable number of applications, you need to take step 3. This involves establishing a point-scoring system for each part of the application. A simple system might look something like this:

Relevant work experience	max. 25 points
Desirable skills and qualifications	max. 25 points
Specific achievements	max. 10 points
Presentation of application	max. 10 points
(Total	max. 70 points)

The idea is to give every applicant a score against each of these criteria. If several people are involved in the shortlisting process, each one provides a separate and confidential score. Add up the total points scored for each candidate. If you plan to interview ten candidates, you then shortlist those with the ten highest scores.

Apart from being a methodical and systematic method of shortlisting, it may also provide supporting evidence in the unlikely event you are challenged on grounds of racial, gender or age discrimination.

Shortlisting matrix

In the three-step approach above, we considered a simple point-scoring method for shortlisting a number of candidates for interview. A more sophisticated method involves looking in more detail at each of the requirements listed in the person specification. List the requirements of the role, in order of importance, down the left column of a sheet of A4.

1 Essential experience/qualifications/skills first.
2 Desirable experience/qualifications/skills second.

Using a copy of this page for each applicant, consider whether or not he or she meets each requirement as follows:

Yes	(meets requirement)
No	(does not meet requirement)
Partial	(partially meets requirement)
Unknown	(not possible to determine from application whether meets requirement or not)

When you have reviewed all the applications, you can count the number of positive matches, and shortlist in this way. Don't forget that positive matches against the essential requirements of the role are more important than those against the desirable requirements. See overleaf.

Screening out unsuitable candidates

Whether you have received a large response to your recruitment drive or not, filtering out the unsuitable candidates is usually easier than identifying the best ones to interview.

Assuming you have compiled a person specification, you already know the essential and desirable attributes, skills and qualifications that you are looking for. So the first step when screening out unsuitable candidates is to reject any candidate who does not meet every essential requirement.

For example, if you are looking for a Fork Lift Truck Operator, you may receive an application from someone who does not have the necessary licence, even though they are very keen and willing to learn. The appropriate licence was an essential requirement of the role, and so this candidate should be filtered out without further consideration.

Shortlisting Criteria	Meets requirement? yes/no/partial/ unknown	Evidence
Knowledge: Of office procedures Of word processing		
Aptitude: Able to understand the need for and maintain confidentiality		
Skills: Word processing (min. 35wpm to be tested) Numeracy and communication skills Organized approach to work Able to prioritize work and manage time		
Experience: Working unsupervised Working as part of a team Providing a confidential secretarial service Delivering a range of high quality administrative services Using word processing, spreadsheets and database packages		
Personal qualities: Able to react calmly under pressure Reliable and conscientious Flexible attitude to work		

sample shortlisting matrix

Gimmicks

For some reason, you will always receive one or two applications from candidates determined to stand out from the rest at any cost. Instead of achieving this by good presentation, or relevant experience, they do it with 'gimmicks'. Believe it or not, here are a few of the methods I have seen used:

- applications presented on paper with stars and glitter
- photographs of the applicants in a state of partial undress
- application forms completed in verse
- supporting letters of endorsement from the parents of applicants
- begging requests for interviews
- applications supported by primary school reports from when the candidates were children.

In all but a very few situations, gimmicky applications should be rejected. These candidates are not taking the role, or your organization, seriously. Humour has its place, but to take a chance with a job application demonstrates a clear lack of judgement on the part of the applicant.

Dealing with a large or small response

If your recruitment drive has been effective so far, you should find that you receive applications only from suitably qualified candidates. Shortlisting can be much harder when the recruitment drive has been less effective, resulting in either too many or too few applications.

If you have received too few applications, you need to ask the following questions:

- Did you advertise the vacancy effectively and in the right media?
- Are the required skills for the role particularly hard to come by?
- Are you offering adequate remuneration?

If the problem relates to where or how you advertised the vacancy, you may simply have to compose an alternatively worded advertisement and re-advertise the position. If you think that the problem lies in the scarcity of candidates with the skills you require, you should consider alternative recruitment sources such as headhunters or search consultants. Perhaps you have just been too demanding with the minimum level of skills and qualifications you are looking for? If so, you may need to re-advertise.

Receiving too many applications can be just as hard to deal with as too few. When faced with hundreds of applications to consider, how can you be sure that you are giving every applicant equal consideration? In many organizations, it just is not possible. But you have to ensure that your selection process is both fair and not discriminatory. So you must apply the same discipline and rigour for a hundred applications as you would for six.

The three-step quick shortlisting method described earlier will help you to filter out the obviously unsuitable candidates, giving you more time to consider the rest. Do not be tempted to reduce your list further by selecting on the basis of the best academic results. There are two reasons for this:

1 Academic performance may not be relevant to the applicant's ability to do the job.
2 Appointing overqualified people to vacancies can lead to poor performance, boredom and high staff turnover.

So stick to the original selection criteria, referring to the person specification, and concentrate on each applicant's match against the essential and desirable skills and qualifications.

You may want to enlist the help of colleagues. They could filter out those applications where the candidate falls short of the essential requirements of the role. This first trawl should then enable you to spend more time on the better suited candidates.

Acknowledging applications

Many organizations do not take the trouble to acknowledge applications for vacancies. They write to invite shortlisted candidates for interview, and when the successful candidate has been appointed they write to all the other applicants to reject them.

Just put yourself in the position of the applicant for a minute. For this purpose, we will call our candidate Jane. She probably spent at least half a day completing her application form, presenting it neatly and posting it to you. She sent it to you one Monday morning, shortly before the closing date that was specified in the advertisement. Meanwhile John, the manager who was recruiting:

- waited until the closing date (1 week)
- considered all the applications he received (1 week)
- wrote to shortlisted candidates inviting them to interview (1 week)
- interviewed the candidates (1 week)
- conducted second interviews (1 week)
- appointed a candidate and followed up references (3 days)
- wrote to reject unsuccessful candidates (1 week).

As one of the unsuccessful candidates, Jane had to wait over six weeks before she heard from John about her application. What's more, this was just one of four jobs that Jane had applied for!

So, make sure that you follow a golden rule – acknowledge each application, as soon after it is received as possible:

1 Date stamp each application as it arrives.
2 Set up a standard letter or acknowledgement.
3 At the end of each week, at the latest, despatch a letter of acknowledgement to every applicant.

Balloon View Ltd
338 Euston Road
London
NW1

Dear Ms Hodgson

Thank you for your application for the post of Supervisor.

We are currently considering all the applications received and we will be in touch with you again shortly.

Yours sincerely

John Maynard

Assessing a CV

We have already considered the benefits of using application forms for potential candidates to complete when applying for a vacancy in your organization (see Chapter 9). Nevertheless, many organizations still request that, initially, applicants submit their curriculum vitae (CV), together with a covering letter. So what should you look for when you are reading through your applications? What can you 'read between the lines'? How will you select for interview from a pile of several hundred CVs?

The CV and covering letter provide you with a snapshot of an applicant. They must grab your attention and compete with all the other applications. They must make you want to interview them to find out more. A CV should cover, simply and effectively, the following information:

- a candidate's qualifications, and how they are relevant to the position you are recruiting for
- a candidate's experience, along with its relevance to your vacancy
- a candidate's skills, as well as how they would be useful to your organization
- a candidate's achievements to date, both personal and in the workplace.

Be realistic about what to expect. You want a CV to grab your attention, but only for the right reasons. Go back to the job description and person specification, and assess how each CV and covering letter address the needs of both the role and the person required to perform it.

Reading between the lines

Gaps in a candidate's employment history may be for entirely legitimate reasons. However, you should look out for attempts to cover up employment history gaps in a candidate's CV. The most obvious way that a candidate might attempt this is by being vague about specific dates of employment. For example:

Watsons Piping Ltd	Field sales operative	1991–1995
BGH Engineering Ltd	Field sales operative	1995–1997
Hallimores Ltd	Sales team leader	1998–2000

At a first reading, you might reasonably assume that this applicant has had a solid employment history in sales for almost ten years. Not necessarily. Suppose the applicant left Watsons in January 1995, and did not join BGH until December. They could have been out of work for almost a full year. You shouldn't dismiss this candidate automatically, particularly if their qualifications and experience match your requirements, but you should certainly make a note to find out more.

Other signs to look out for

A career gap is just one of the signs you are looking for when assessing a CV. How stable does the applicant's career path appear to be? Would you say that there has been a logical progression between jobs, or has the applicant swapped careers on more than one occasion?

If use of English is important to the vacancy you are trying to fill, take a look at how the CV is written. More than one spelling mistake would indicate clumsiness, or lack of care. After all, every word processor comes with a spell checker. How appropriate is the language used in the CV? Has the applicant listed relevant experience and qualifications only? A long-winded, poorly phrased CV might indicate that the applicant either does not have the relevant experience, or that he/she finds it hard to get to the point. What about presentation? Again, even with a low specification word processor, someone with little design flair can easily create a simple, clearly laid out document. If the CV in front of you is poorly presented, you might conclude that the applicant is prone to rushing things, or not demonstrating care. Be patient when working through a pile of applications. Any one of these signs, in isolation, might not be critical. But be on your guard nonetheless. A CV that is poorly laid out, with spelling mistakes and career gaps, is probably best rejected.

As you read through each CV, jot down questions that you will want to ask of the applicant if they are selected for interview. You could also record one or two key facts so that you can quickly remind yourself about each applicant. Above all, remember that a CV is only a two-dimensional representation of a candidate. It is extremely hard to get an accurate picture of a candidate from a CV and covering letter alone.

Covering letters

A covering letter gives you the opportunity to see whether the applicant is able to follow a simple set of instructions. Look at it and ask yourself the following questions:

1 Has the applicant correctly spelt your name, the name of your organization, and the full address where the application was sent?
2 Did the applicant correctly quote the right reference (where applicable)?
3 Does the covering letter refer specifically to the job they are

applying for, or does it read like a mass-produced letter that could be used to apply for any vacancy in any organization?

4   If you requested a hand-written letter, did the applicant supply one, or did they type it? It may sound harsh, but this is a classic example of where an applicant has failed to follow a simple instruction.

5   Does the covering letter make you want to meet the applicant? Does any of the applicant's personality come across in the letter?

6   Does the covering letter enhance their CV, or does it merely repeat or paraphrase sections from it?

The answers to these questions should indicate whether you should reject the application, or retain it for further consideration. At this stage, you are not necessarily trying to produce a final shortlist, but you are trying to filter out unsuitable applications as early in the recruitment process as possible.

Inviting to interview

The way that you invite candidates to interview partly depends on the interview method that you choose. You may, for example, conduct first interviews on the telephone. If you decide to conduct face-to-face interviews, it is customary to write to shortlisted candidates in the first instance. The wording of the letter should be simple and reasonably brief.

In addition to a map, and any publicity material you have, you should make sure that your shortlisted candidates are sent a job description and person specification, if they have not seen them already.

You may find that one or two of your shortlisted candidates turn down the offer of an interview. They may have been offered alternative employment since their application, or they may simply have changed their minds about working for your organization. If this happens, move on to your reserve list and invite an alternative candidate for interview.

Balloon View Ltd
338 Euston Road
London
NW1

Dear Ms Hodgson

Thank you for your application for the post of Supervisor.

I am writing to invite you to interview at 9.00 a.m. on Wednesday 23 August at our main offices on the Euston Road.

The interview should last no more than one hour, and will be conducted by me, together with Jim Swanton, our Head of Personnel.

I enclose a map, together with directions for how to find us, as well as a copy of our current brochure.

Please note that we will reimburse any travelling expenses that you incur. I would be grateful if you would confirm your availability by telephoning my secretary, Alison, on 020 8776 2345.

I look forward to meeting you.

Yours sincerely

John Maynard
Customer Services Division

Rejecting unsuitable candidates

The delicate process of rejecting candidates is considered in some detail in Chapter 19. In brief, it is essential that you write to candidates that you do not plan to employ as soon as you are able. A sample letter is laid out below.

[Current Date]

Dear *[Salutation]*,

I am writing to you regarding your recent application for the position of *[Job Title]* with *[Company Name]*.

We received an excellent response to our advertisement and unfortunately we will not be taking your application any further on this occasion.

I would like to take this opportunity to wish you every success in your future career. Thank you for your interest in *[Company Name]*.

Yours sincerely

[First Name] *[Surname]*
[Job Title]

Checklist

✓ How many candidates do you propose to shortlist for interview?

✓ Can you remember the three-step process for shortlisting?

✓ Would a shortlisting matrix help you to compile a suitable shortlist?

✓ Can you screen out unsuitable candidates quickly and effectively?

✓ Would you spot a 'gimmicky' application?

✓ Are you equipped to handle a larger than expected response?

✓ Would you know what to do if you received too few applications?

✓ Have you remembered to acknowledge all applications, as soon as you receive them?

✓ Could you assess a candidate's CV effectively?

✓ Would you know how to 'read between the lines' in an application?

✓ Do you know how and when to invite shortlisted candidates for interview?

✓ Are you ready to reject unsuitable candidates?

part

four

the interview

preparing for interview

In this chapter you will learn:

- where to interview
- when to interview
- who should conduct the interview.

So now you have identified *who* you plan to interview, the next question to consider is *how*? There are several types of interview you could conduct, involving various people in your organization. What interview methods are available to you, and how should you go about organizing them?

Types of interview

There are a number of ways to interview candidates, and the method you choose might depend on:

- the number of people involved in the interview process
- the number of people you propose to interview
- the size and culture of your organization.

Here are the main interview methods you might use, and guidance on the most appropriate time to use them.

Telephone interviews

Often you will end up with a larger shortlist than you would like. In such circumstances it is a good idea to use a preliminary interview method to screen out unsuitable candidates, and to decide who you would like to interview face to face. One way to do this is to contact each person on your shortlist by telephone.

Do not be afraid to use the telephone as an interviewing tool. It can play a very important role in the selection process. First impressions count for a lot, and the way that a candidate talks and uses the telephone might influence your selection, particularly if the role requires a lot of telephone calling. However, there are two vital rules to bear in mind when telephoning candidates:

1   Never ever offer someone a job on the basis of a telephone interview alone. You should always meet a candidate face to face first, even if it is for just a short period.
2   Use discretion and caution when telephoning candidates at their current place of work. Be prepared to phone candidates at home outside normal working hours. If you do not have a home telephone number for a candidate you may call them at work, ask them if it is convenient to talk, and arrange a mutually convenient time and place to conduct a preliminary telephone interview. If you reach the company switchboard first, do whatever you can to be put through to the candidate without disclosing from where you are calling. It is likely that

the candidate will not want their current employer to know that they are job hunting, and you should respect this at all times.

Remember what you are trying to achieve by telephoning candidates. Your objective is to screen out unsuitable candidates. Ensure that you make this clear to candidates when you phone them. You could begin the conversation by saying something like: 'I am telephoning a number of candidates who broadly meet our requirements. I want to tell you a bit more about the vacancy, and to raise one or two issues regarding your application. We will then write to shortlisted candidates to invite them for an interview at our office.'

The telephone provides an ideal forum for gauging a first impression of a candidate. As the call progresses, make notes about how the candidate performs on the telephone. Are they confident? Are they nervous? Polite? Would you say that they have good verbal communication skills? Try to imagine this person representing your organization. If you were a client, would you be impressed talking to this person? This is an important consideration, especially when the vacancy concerned requires someone with good communication skills.

A telephone interview is also good for confirming basic facts. For example, you could confirm qualifications, grades, and details of gaps in a candidate's CV.

It is important that you plan and prepare for a telephone interview as thoroughly as you would a face-to-face interview. A preliminary telephone interview provides the opportunity to start building rapport with a candidate, and you will not be able to do this if you are unprepared. So think about what you want to ask beforehand, and remain calm and polite throughout. Remember that you will both be nervous.

There are a number of ways to conclude a telephone interview. The candidate may decide that they are not interested or qualified for the role, in which case you should thank them for their time and wish them well. Alternatively, you may conclude that the candidate is not appropriate for the role, in which case you could end the conversation by saying one of the following things:

1 The position requires someone with more experience in (a particular field), but I will keep your details on file for other vacancies for which you may be more suited.

2 I need to discuss your application with my colleagues. I will be back in touch shortly.

If you decide on the second option, make sure that you do as you say. Either write to the candidate, or telephone them again straight away.

You may decide that you wish to interview the candidate face to face in which case you should tell them that you will contact them shortly to arrange a suitable time and venue for interview.

Although it can be awkward to raise the issue of salary, you could save yourself a great deal of time and expense if you bring the subject up at this stage. You may be faced with an ideal candidate who has considerably higher expectations of salary than you can offer. It is better to know this earlier than after one or two rounds of interviews.

Face-to-face interviews

As the term suggests, these involve *one* interviewer and *one* interviewee. Traditionally they are the most common form of job interview. They are easy to organize, and are often fairly relaxed and informal. You can build rapport more quickly with a candidate if it is just the two of you.

If you are not an experienced interviewer, one-to-one interviews can be hard work. They can be stressful, with long pauses between questions. But even if you are experienced you should bear two points in mind:

1 You have no one to share your thoughts or opinions with about a particular candidate.
2 Inevitably, you will form a very personal and subjective view of a candidate.

Nevertheless, one-to-one interviews are popular and they can play an important role in the selection process.

Panel interviews

Panel interviews involve two or more interviewers with each interviewee. In some public sector organizations, panels might include 20 or more participants. Normally, each of the interviewers has a specific role to play. The panel might consist of:

- a member of the personnel department
- the head of the department in which the vacancy occurs

- the appropriate line manager
- someone with a particular specialist interest (e.g. finance)
- a member of the senior management team.

Collectively, the panel takes a *team* approach. There are two key advantages to this method of interviewing.

1 A broad range of strengths and skills is represented amongst the panel. Each member of the panel can ask the candidate questions relating to their specialist interest.
2 As a team, you can form a much more objective view of a candidate's ability and suitability for the role.

However, there are disadvantages. Panel interviews are often difficult to arrange, with several diaries needing to be co-ordinated. A lot of business time is lost, with so many key staff removed from their daily schedules. Panel interviews are also difficult to structure, with each interviewer wanting to ask their own questions. The candidate may feel daunted when faced with so many personalities, each with their own agenda.

If you use panel interviews, make sure that all the interviewers are thoroughly prepared. Distribute the candidate's application to all members of the panel well in advance of the interview. It is hard to structure a panel interview, and it will be even harder if members of the panel are inadequately briefed.

Serial interviews

Serial interviews comprise several one-to-one interviews in succession. Someone with a specialist interest conducts each of the interviews. A candidate may move from interview to interview in a single day, or over a number of days.

This is a good method for reducing your shortlist, because candidates might drop out at any of the interview stages. For example, a candidate might fall short of the organization's requirements during a financial interview and will not be required to attend further interview stages.

With this technique, you can include problem solving or role play stages if you wish, and over the complete cycle of interviews you get to view a candidate from a number of different perspectives. Serial interviews require the same amount of planning and organization as panel interviews, but each interviewer is given the chance to judge the candidate independently against their own criteria. One of the key benefits of this type of interview is that if you suspect that a candidate is prone to a certain weakness, you can ask the next interviewer to probe it further.

Self-selecting interviews

This is an unusual interviewing technique that is best reserved for recruiting for roles that are particularly pressured or demanding, such as target-driven sales positions. However much you emphasize the skills required in a recruitment advertisement, you will often find yourself with a large number of similar applications, with little on paper to choose between them. On occasions like this, turn the interview process on its head and invite all the candidates to attend an open meeting at a certain time and date.

Use the open meeting to tell all the candidates about the role. Use the forum to explain the dedication and long hours that the position requires. Get candidates into groups and act out some role play selling situations. You should divide the meeting up into a number of 20-minute sessions, each with a different focus. Tell the candidates that they are free to leave at any stage if they decide that the job is not for them. Some will not want to put in the hours. Others will not want to participate in the role play. Some will see better-qualified candidates amongst them, and will leave before they are rejected. Over the course of the meeting candidates will drop out. Remember that, for a sales role, you are looking for the person who will stand out from the crowd, and you will have plenty of opportunity to spot them during the interview sessions.

By the end, you will have a shortlist that is manageable. Invite those who have stayed back for a face-to-face second interview, and make your selection from amongst them.

Multi-group interviews

This is when two or more interviewers meet with two or more shortlisted candidates. This method of interviewing is rarely used, but it can be very effective, particularly when gauging how candidates are likely to act as part of a team. You should not ask personal or factual questions about a candidate if other candidates are present. Instead, you should address situational or hypothetical questions to the candidates as a group, and note how they respond. Some candidates will try to dominate the conversation, while others will take a more measured approach. Some may even attempt to argue with another candidate's view, trying to make them look foolish. It can be a very enlightening experience, and you should watch very carefully how each of the candidates responds.

You will need to interview the candidates individually as well, so this multi-group approach is best performed at the second or subsequent interview stage.

Where to interview?

Choosing an appropriate venue for an interview will take some thought. It is an important consideration, as the right venue will put a candidate at ease and will ensure that they perform at their best. Think about the options open to you. These might include:

- office
- meeting room
- boardroom
- hotel room
- hotel foyer
- restaurant.

The choice of venue will depend on the type of interview you are conducting, the impression you want the interviewee to have of your organization, and the discretion or confidentiality that is appropriate.

On the whole, interviews conducted in your office are more formal, whilst those held in restaurants or hotel foyers are less so. Only you can decide the right venue for your interviews, but wherever you choose to interview, you should bear the following points in mind:

- Make sure that the sun is not shining in the candidate's eyes.
- Ensure that you are not disturbed: Put the telephone on divert if you can. Switch off your mobile. Leave a *do not disturb* sign on the door. Let colleagues know that you are interviewing. Interruptions are disruptive to both you and the candidate.
- Get the temperature right. Try to strike a balance between warmth and a supply of fresh air.
- Offer candidates a drink. If you are interviewing several candidates in succession, you may not want to make tea or coffee each time. As a bare minimum keep a jug of fresh water available throughout the interview. Biscuits or sandwiches are not a good idea unless you are conducting the interview in a restaurant. It is very hard to eat and talk at the same time.

Venue	Advantages	Disadvantages
Your own office	• Convenient • Cost-effective • Candidate gets to see working environment	• Formal atmosphere that might make the candidate feel uncomfortable • Cluttered or untidy
Meeting room/ boardroom	• Quiet • Uncluttered	• Cold or bare • A bit formal
Hotel foyer	• Convenient • Discreet • Plenty of facilities available (tea/ coffee)	• Does not give the candidate any impression of the working environment • Plenty of distractions
Hotel room	• Hotel staff may meet and greet candidates • Plenty of facilities available (tea/ coffee) • No disturbances • Good for inter-viewing several candidates in a short period	• Characterless • Does not give the candidate any impression of the working environment

- Think about seating. Unless you particularly want to create a formal atmosphere, try not to sit face to face across a desk. Sitting around a coffee table or work table will put the candidate more at ease. A table of some sort, however, is a good idea. You will both need something to rest on, and you will not spend the interview crossing and uncrossing your legs.
- Make sure that both you and the candidate are sitting in chairs at the same height. From a candidate's point of view, it is extremely intimidating to be sitting much lower than the person you are talking to.

When to interview?

Once you have decided upon where you will conduct interviews, the next consideration is when. What is the most suitable day of the week? What is the best time of day?

Think about the candidates you are interviewing. Are they mostly in full-time employment already? If so, they may be glad to be interviewed first thing in the morning, or at the end of the day. Often they will not want to arouse suspicion at their current employment, and it may be easier to ask for time off at either end of the working day. You should be sympathetic to this request when arranging interview times with candidates.

What about working parents? They may prefer an interview time in the middle of the morning, once they have dropped children off at school. For local applicants, a lunchtime interview might be perfect. Everyone is different, and you should be flexible when arranging an interview schedule. Apart from anything else, candidates will not perform well if they know they should be somewhere else. If they come to an interview with a clear conscience, they are likely to perform at their best.

Planning an interview schedule takes time, and may involve several attempts. Don't forget that it is not only the candidate's wishes that need to be taken into account. Often, two or more people will conduct the interviews, so you need to find suitable times when all interviewers are available. Make sure that there is someone who is responsible for leading the interview. An interview where no one has prepared sufficiently can be extremely embarrassing, and will give the candidate a poor impression of the organization.

Other rules you should try to follow regarding the timing of interviews are:

- Hold interviews at times when you will not be disturbed. It is unacceptable to break out of interviews in order to take phone calls, however important.
- Allow anything between 45 and 90 minutes for each interview. Any longer than 90 minutes, and you should not expect candidates to keep their concentration.
- Leave time between interviews for a brief discussion with the other interviewers, to make notes about the candidate, and to catch up with any urgent business that may have arisen.
- Do not try to interview too many candidates in a single day. About four or five one-hour interviews is about right.

Who should interview?

The answer to this question will depend largely on the nature of the organization that you work for. In many larger organizations, for example, it is mandatory for a member of the personnel department to be present at all recruitment interviews. Nevertheless, there are a number of factors you should consider when deciding who should be involved in the interview process.

- If the position is a key one within your team or department, should your superior or team leader attend?
- If the new recruit will report to two or more people, why not make sure that all are available to attend the interview?
- If the employee is likely to spend part of their time working closely with another team, department or division, why not suggest that one of its representatives attends?
- If you are not an experienced interviewer, should you ask for support from a colleague who is?

For most interviews, it is relatively straightforward to identify who would assist most by attending. If you are responsible for managing the new employee on a daily or regular basis, then clearly you should attend. If your superior has overall responsibility for the team or department, then he or she should probably also attend, although they may prefer to take part only at the second interview stage. A more junior colleague, who will have to work closely with the new employee, can provide an excellent second opinion. A representative from the Human Resources or Personnel Department, may be required. The important point to note is that if there is more than one interviewer, a leader should be appointed. Other interviewers may ask questions at any time, but there is always one person who steers the interview right from the beginning.

Checklist

✓ Which type of interview do you plan to conduct?
✓ Do you need to conduct preliminary interviews over the telephone?
✓ Where will your interviews take place?
✓ How will you arrange the room in which you interview candidates?
✓ Have you made sure you will not be disturbed?
✓ Have you plenty of water and/or other refreshments available?

✓ Will your interview location be formal or informal?
✓ What time of day will you interview?
✓ Who will conduct the interviews? Just you? Your colleagues? Someone from the Human Resources department?

12

starting the interview

In this chapter you will learn:

- how to greet and relax candidates
- how to build rapport
- how to prepare for the interview.

So, you have chosen an interview method, and have invited shortlisted candidates for interview. Your colleagues are ready, the interview room is set up, and the candidates are beginning to arrive. First impressions count for you and the interviewee, so what do you need to do to make sure the interview starts well?

Greeting and relaxing candidates

As candidates arrive for interview, make sure that there is someone on hand to greet them. A candidate is likely to feel nervous on arrival, and it creates an unfavourable impression if they are kept waiting in an empty reception area.

Waiting for an interview is never a pleasant experience. Ask whoever greets the candidate to offer them a glass of water, or tea or coffee if the wait is likely to be longer than a few minutes. Have some company literature handy for the candidate to read, or get them started on any forms or tests that you want them to complete. Now is as good a time as any to sort out administrative details like reimbursing travel expenses, if appropriate.

When you are ready to interview, go and meet the candidate yourself. Don't send someone else on your behalf unless they are also part of the interviewing team. On meeting the candidate, be polite and direct. Introduce yourself, saying something positive like: 'Hello. I'm Peter Harris. We spoke on the phone.'

A short walk along a corridor will seem like a mile to a nervous candidate, so try to fill the silence as you both walk to the interview room. You do not need to practise your small talk, but try asking about where the candidate has come from, how their journey was, or anything else that might break the ice initially. Once in the interview room, show the candidate where they should sit. It is not always obvious. By all means offer the candidate a drink, but a glass or jug of fresh water is probably sufficient. Making tea or coffee will either mean leaving the candidate on their own for another five minutes, or an interruption during the interview when it is delivered. Offering biscuits or sandwiches during an interview is not a good idea. It is difficult to listen, talk and eat at the same time. Imagine the embarrassment if you, or the candidate, spat food whilst saying something.

Building rapport

The skill of the first few minutes of the interview is to relax the candidate, and to build rapport with them as quickly as you can. You could start by outlining the structure of the interview. If there are several interviews or tests involved, you could describe these briefly. You might want to refer to the number of applications you have received, and the number of candidates you propose to interview. You are giving the candidate an idea of how far they have come already, and about what lies ahead. If they are particularly nervous, you might want to put them at ease by starting straight away with a positive statement or question arising from their CV or application form. For example: 'I see from your CV that you enjoy playing for the local football team. What position do you play? How are the team doing this season?'

You might even want to refer to their state of mind directly: 'I remember being eaten up with nerves at my first job interview, so I can imagine how you are feeling right now.'

You could also start with something positive that they have achieved: 'I see you completed your Diploma in marketing from the Chartered Institute of Marketing. You did well to find the time for this, while you were working full-time at Longbridges.'

The rule is very simple. The quicker your candidate relaxes, the more productive the interview will be. Even the most qualified candidates get stage fright, and can come across as totally unsuitable for the job. So do not neglect this important part of the interview process.

There are books devoted to the subject of building rapport, so you are unlikely to crack it from these paragraphs alone. However, your goal is to make the candidate act as naturally as they can, so that you see them as they really are. It is much easier to interview someone who is behaving naturally, rather than acting like the person they think you are looking for. If you can make the candidate relax, and speak up, it will help you decide more quickly whether or not they are the right person for the job.

Being prepared

There is no excuse for not preparing thoroughly in advance of the interview. Beforehand you should have reminded yourself why you shortlisted the candidate, noted the questions that you plan to ask and begun to consider where their strengths and weaknesses lie. You should not need to pore over the candidate's application form or CV during the course of the interview, apart from towards the end when you are making sure that you have covered all the points you intended to raise. Poor preparation will be obvious to the candidate, and will make them think twice about working for you. Signs of poor preparation include:

- asking factual questions that have already been addressed within the CV or application form (e.g. 'Which university did you go to?', 'What did you study?')
- reading through the candidate's application in order to find questions to ask
- long and embarrassing pauses between questions
- asking a series of unrelated questions, jumping from topic to topic
- neglecting to ask a question about an obvious shortcoming that might affect the candidate's ability to do the job (e.g. 'The role requires a degree of book-keeping, and I don't think you have mentioned book-keeping in your application. Do you have any basic management accounting experience?').

Any of these will give the candidate reason to think that you do not take their application very seriously. They may even decide that they will turn down a job offer from you if you make one. Simple preparation will make you and the candidate feel more comfortable throughout the interview.

Checklist

✓ Has the person covering reception greeted the interviewee politely?

✓ Do you know how to relax an interviewee as you meet them for the first time?

✓ Could you engage the interviewee in small talk while you walk to the interview room?

✓ Are you any good at building rapport?

✓ Are you sufficiently prepared that you could ask a candidate an appropriate question without referring to their application?

13

questioning techniques

In this chapter you will learn:

- how to prepare questions
- about the different types of questions you might ask
- how to keep questions up your sleeve.

So, the candidate is taking his/her seat in the interview room. The application is in front of you and the interview is about to begin. Do you feel prepared? Do you know the types of questions to ask? Would you know what to do if the conversation dries up?

Question preparation

It is almost eleven o'clock. Your telephone rings, and it is the receptionist telling you that a candidate has arrived for an interview. You had planned to spend some time this morning preparing for it, but other urgent tasks got in the way. You ask someone to show the candidate into the meeting room to give you time to run through their CV. You buy a bit more time by offering the candidate a large mug of tea or coffee while they wait. You have about five minutes to run through their CV, try to remember why you shortlisted them in the first place, and consider what questions you are going to ask them. But it does not matter too much. After all, you are bound to think of some questions during the course of the interview.

The importance of preparation

If this is you, then you are not alone. But as with all aspects of the recruitment process, the key to good interview questioning is preparation. The cost to the organization of recruiting the wrong person is substantial, both financially and emotionally, and so it is essential that you use the interview process wisely.

Consider why you are conducting interviews. What does an interview add to the recruitment process that a CV or application form will not provide? A well-planned interview will:

- reveal more information about a candidate than the summary provided in a CV
- add new information that is missing from the CV
- encourage the candidate to open up and talk, giving you the opportunity to assess them in terms of their ability, skills and personality.

You ought to be using the interview process to answer the following questions about each person that you interview:

- Can this person do the job?
- Will this person fit into the team, and into the organization as a whole?

- Will this person want to work for us?
- Will this person be a reliable and dedicated employee?

The danger of interviewing without proper preparation is that you will only find answers to some of these questions. When you are comparing two candidates after the first round of interviews, you will not be able to do so in a fair and balanced way. So make sure that you prepare for each interview thoroughly.

Consider the complete application

When you made your shortlist of people to interview, you carefully assessed each candidate's CV or application form against the job and person specifications. Now is the time to go back through the notes that you made, and consider the questions that you will ask each candidate at interview.

Looking at a candidate's CV or application form, remind yourself of the reasons why you decided to interview them. Consider what further information you would like to have about this person, and write down some questions you could ask that will help you. Examples might include:

- gaps in career history
- skills/experience referred to that you would like to know more about
- skills/experience implied, but not stated
- skills/experience required for the job, but not stated on the CV/application form
- hobbies and interests – what does this person do outside work?
- education – why did this person study a particular course?

You should also refer to the job and person specifications when preparing questions for interview. Comparing these two documents with the CV or application form, where does this person fall short of the requirements of the role? Where are they overqualified? Make notes on questions you could ask at interview that would confirm these.

Balancing questions

Remember that an interview is more than just an opportunity to ask a series of questions. Listening is just as important, and you will think of other questions that you want to ask resulting from the answers you receive. So preparation is about making sure you do not miss something important, rather than about planning every single question you will ask during the interview. A good interview will flow logically and progressively, and your questioning route should reflect this.

Once you have made notes on the questions you would like to ask, ensure that the list is balanced. In other words, it should include some questions that require short factual answers, and others that will get a candidate thinking and talking. Some different types of question are described below.

Closed questions

Closed questions are questions that demand a one-word answer, or a very short response. Examples include:

Q Can you use Microsoft Word?
A Yes, I can.

Q Can you speak Italian?
A No, I can't.

Q What is your typing speed?
A 60 words per minute.

An inexperienced interviewer will often ask too many closed questions, and may conclude that the interviewee does not have much to say. So you should remember that closed questions are best used when checking basic information about a candidate. Perhaps there is something that was not made clear in their CV or application form. For example:

Q In which month did you leave Morrisons?
Q How many years have you worked at Simpsons?
Q How long is your notice period?
Q Are you able to work evening and weekend shifts?

You may also need to use closed questions with certain types of candidate. For example, when interviewing someone who will not stop talking, in order to break up what they are saying. Or with a candidate whom you suspect of being vague or evasive with their answers. For example:

Q So when *exactly* was this?
Q Did you resign from this post, or were you asked to leave?

The important thing is to strike a balance between open and closed questions. Allow plenty of opportunity for the candidate to have their say. But make sure you uncover the important facts as well. Do not be afraid of asking a closed question in order to be certain of a particular point.

Open questions

Open questions are much broader, and demand a longer answer. You use these to invite a discussion and to get a candidate talking. The candidate will need to consider their response to each open question, and will not be able to hide behind a short or one-word answer.

Open questions often begin with one of the 'W' words: Who? Why? What? When? For example:

Q What do you like most about your current position? What do you like least?
Q Why do you feel you are particularly suited to this position?
Q What do you hope to achieve by changing jobs at this time?
Q Who do you go to for help or guidance?

But there are also other ways to begin open questions in order to start a longer discussion, or to really get a candidate thinking. For example:

Q Tell me about some of the challenges you face in your current job.
Q How do you handle stress in your work?
Q How did you get the information you needed from the senior managers?

Open questions reveal a lot more about a candidate than closed questions. With open questions, it is harder for candidates simply to provide the answer that they think you want to hear. So you will learn a lot more about a candidate's ability, personality and skills by considering carefully the open questions that you ask.

If you are well prepared then you will have considered several open and closed questions to ask before the interview has begun, and plenty more will present themselves during the interview itself.

Situational questions

A situational question is when you outline a hypothetical situation to a candidate, and ask them how they would deal with it.

For example:

Q Suppose you had two pieces of work to finish by midday, one for your immediate superior, and one for the Managing Director. It is clear you will not meet the deadline for both tasks. What would you do?

Q You suspect that a colleague is stealing from the till. You know that he/she has money problems at the moment. How would you deal with this situation?

Q Suppose a customer telephoned you, complaining that they felt ill after eating one of the company's products. How would you react?

The situations you use should, as far as possible, reflect typical scenarios that the job holder is likely to face. You will then get a revealing insight into the way a candidate might deal with a particular situation. However, you should use situational questions with a degree of caution. Remember that a candidate will have little or no direct knowledge of how the organization operates, or even of the industry that the organization operates in. So you should judge the response you get by the approach that the candidate would take, rather than look for a perfect answer.

Leading questions

Leading questions are ones that suggest or imply a particular answer. For example:

Q Presumably, if a member of your team were rude to a customer, you would dismiss them on the spot?

A Yes, absolutely.

Q You're not suggesting that qualifications are less important than experience are you?

A No, of course not.

Asking leading questions is hardly ever effective in an interview situation. You rarely learn more about a candidate by leading them to a particular response. They can be useful, however, if you suspect a candidate of consistently giving you answers that they think you want to hear. In these circumstances it is legitimate to throw in a leading question as bait, and see if they hook themselves.

Creating stress

You often hear about interviewers who are particularly tough, or who seem to enjoy intimidating candidates. Whilst it is never recommended to make a candidate feel uneasy just for the sake of it, there are occasions when creating stress in an interview is very important.

Dealing with stress has become a part of working life. There is stress in every job nowadays, but some careers and roles are particularly stressful by their very nature (for example, any role handling customer complaints). When recruiting for a position that requires a calm, unflappable person, it is legitimate to create stress in the interview to see how the candidate reacts. You can do this by challenging some of the answers that the candidate gives to the questions you ask. For example:

Q Are you really suggesting that you would tolerate a team member who was not pulling their weight?
Q How on earth do you manage to do your current job without spreadsheet skills?

The aim is simply to see how the candidate reacts to being challenged. A candidate who deals with stress effectively will remain calm under such questioning. That is all you are looking for, so once you have established this, progress the interview on a calmer footing.

Probing questions

Probing questions are used to obtain additional detail from the candidate by delving deeper into a topic being discussed. As a result, they often follow on from open questions. For example:

Q (Open)   Why do you want to work in the public sector?
Q (Probing) Don't you feel that your commercial skills are better suited to the private sector?

A probing question is sometimes tough, but always fair. It should sound conversational, and follow seamlessly from the question that preceded it. If you take this care, you may get a more emotive response from the candidate, revealing more about the person and the way that they approach a given situation. If you are not careful, probing questions can sound intrusive and make the candidate feel uncomfortable.

Questions to keep up your sleeve

Any interview can dry up, no matter how well prepared you are. You may have misinterpreted a person's work experience from their CV, or they may have misunderstood the nature of the vacancy. In either case, you could find yourself with a prepared list of questions that are suddenly no longer relevant. So it is a good idea to have a reserve list of questions you could ask of any candidate, just in case you need them. Every job and organization is different, but some examples might include:

1 How would your current work colleagues describe you?
2 What do you think you would contribute to this organization?
3 What do you dislike most about your current position?
4 Where would you like to be in three years' time?
5 Describe your perfect working day.
6 Describe a situation at work where you demonstrated your team skills.
7 What is your greatest weakness?
8 What would you most like to change in your current role?
9 How do you keep yourself motivated?
10 What gives you most job satisfaction in your current role?

Talking too much

A common problem for interviewers, not interviewees, is that they talk too much. It is common for an interviewer to begin the interview by telling the applicant all about the organization. Then they spend ten minutes talking about the job itself, followed by a summary of how the job relates to other positions within the company. Before they realize it, half the time allotted to the interview has passed, and there is just a little time left to ask the applicant a few basic questions. You must remember that your role in the interview process is to learn as much about the applicant's suitability as you can. The applicant has probably already seen a job description, a person specification and any other details about the company that you sent them before the interview. So there is no need to spend much time in the interview process describing the organization and the position to the applicant in detail. You can quickly summarize these details, or leave them to a second or subsequent interview. Let the applicant convince you of their suitability for the role, not the other way round. There should always be a sensible balance. Allow the applicant to talk, but keep him or her on course by asking sensible questions.

Checklist

✓ Are you fully prepared for the interview?
✓ Do you know what types of question you could ask?
✓ Have you thought about specific questions you will ask each candidate?
✓ Have you got a spare question up your sleeve just in case?
✓ Can you think of questions to ask that might get a quiet candidate talking?
✓ Do you know how to create stress in an interview intentionally?
✓ Would you feel confident stopping a candidate from talking too much?

interview style

In this chapter you will learn:

- how to structure your interviews
- about different interview styles
- about the roles you and your colleagues can play during the interview.

Having considered the various ways you can ask questions, it is now time to look at different interview styles. If you have ever been interviewed yourself, you will know that interviews vary considerably in the way they are conducted. Some seem more like informal chats than interviews, whilst others are very formal and sombre. Interviews can be friendly, or they can deliberately create stress. So when is each interview style appropriate, and which is best for you?

Informal or unstructured interviews

It is common in small organizations to adopt an unstructured interview process. Particularly if you are interviewing alone, it might seem sensible to allow the interview just to 'flow', and you might feel tempted to ask questions as they occur to you. You probably trust yourself to cover the ground with each candidate, and you might feel that you are more likely to 'get to know' a candidate in a less formal interview situation.

However accustomed you are to thinking on your feet, be careful. There are lots of pitfalls associated with unstructured interviews:

- They are hard to control, and to keep to a specific time limit.
- You are likely to miss out an important question to ask of every candidate.
- You may feel instinctively drawn to a particular candidate without having the factual evidence to support your choice.
- You may come away from the interviews without feeling able to appoint any candidate.
- You are more likely to have long periods of silence in your interviews while you consider what questions to ask.

Nevertheless, an informal interview can work well in certain situations. For example, you may feel that the informal interview might be the best forum to bring a particularly nervous candidate out of his shell. Is he inherently nervous, or just nervous at interview? If you can relax him with an informal interview, then he may be worth considering. You might have rejected him at a formal or structured interview without establishing the cause of his nerves.

Another good use of the informal interview is to reduce a shortlist. If you have 20 or more good candidates, you could give each of them a 30 minute informal interview in order to reduce the shortlist to the six or eight required for a more formal, structured interview.

Formal or structured interviews

A structured interview style ensures that you treat all candidates in the same way, and that you ask roughly the same questions, in the same order. A typical interview structure might look as follows:

- Welcome:
  Introduce the interviewers to the candidate. Break the ice with a little small talk. Invite the candidate to sit down.
- Interview outline:
  Discuss briefly the structure of the interview with the candidate. How long will the interview be? Will there be any tests to complete? Will the candidate be given the opportunity to ask questions at the end?
- Question exchange:
  Ask the questions that relate to this candidate's match against the person specification. Start with a few 'open' questions that will get the candidate talking. Also ask some of the challenging questions that you plan to ask every candidate.
- Information:
  Give the candidate the chance to ask questions that he or she may have. Is there anything else they need to know about either the job or the organization? This is a good opportunity to establish whether the candidate has done any research about your organization. Are they asking questions about topics that are freely covered on your website, for example?
- Close:
  Discuss briefly the next stage. If invited for further interview, when is this likely to be? When do you plan to make a decision about the appointment?

A formal interview is likely to use a list of pre-planned questions that will be asked of every candidate. Some argue that there is less room for spontaneity and creativity in a formal interview, but they do make sure that you treat every candidate equally, and have an objective means of comparing candidates with one another.

Interview roles

If you are interviewing on your own, you need to plan well and keep a checklist of all the questions you want to ask, and the points you want to raise, with each candidate. You alone will determine how formal the interview will be, and the style that you plan to adopt.

If there is a colleague, or group of colleagues, who can take part in the interviewing and selection process then so much the better. We discussed the ideal interview panel in Chapter 11. With two or more interviewers, each of you can take a different specific role during the interview. There are two common interview roles that you might want to adopt:

Good cop

The good cop is the 'nice guy'. He or she is the person who takes responsibility for greeting the candidate, putting them at their ease, and asking the gentle, easier questions. The good cop will ask about the candidate's journey, and during the interview will pick up on the positive aspects of their application.

Bad cop

The bad cop's role is to act as a contrast to the good cop. Their role is to identify the gaps in the candidate's CV, and ask the more difficult, challenging questions. They often create pressure and stress during the interview, to see how well the candidate handles it. If a candidate struggles to answer a question, the good cop will come to their rescue and phrase the question in a less demanding way. The bad cop won't. They will enjoy the silence and wait for the candidate to come up with their answer. The bad cop is rarely a nasty person, he or she is simply performing an important interview role. If a job is full of pressure and stress, you need to be certain that your preferred candidate can handle it. The bad cop can help you to find out if they can.

The candidates themselves are often unaware of the role playing that is going on. An interviewee might emerge from the interview saying that he got on well with one of the interviewers, but that the other one obviously didn't like him. This may or may not be true, but is a classic example of how a candidate perceives the good cop/bad cop dynamic.

Checklist

✓ Will you conduct formal or informal interviews?
✓ Have you considered the various roles that each interviewer could play?
✓ Which role will you be playing?

15

observation

In this chapter you will learn:

- about body language and what it says about the candidate
- how to listen to what the candidate is saying to you
- how to control an interview
- how to bring an interview to a close.

The interview is well and truly underway. Although what the candidate says is very important, there are other signals that they give off. What does their body language tell you? Are you listening attentively to what they are saying? Observation of both spoken and silent communication is vital during the interview.

Body language

Body language can tell you a great deal about a candidate, and can tell the candidate a great deal about you. Let's start with the signals you subconsciously give to the candidate.

Arms folded

As a general rule, if you fold your arms and lean back you come across as 'closed'. It implies that you are not really listening, or interested, in what the candidate is saying to you.

Head tilted

If you tilt your head away from a candidate when listening to them it implies distrust. If you do not look the candidate in the eye, the distrust is even more pronounced.

Crossed legs

It is said that crossing your legs implies defensiveness.

Clock watching and yawning

It goes without saying that you should never yawn in front of a candidate. You may need to check the progress of an interview periodically, but avoid looking at your watch every few minutes.

Reflection

You might want to give the candidate the impression you are thinking about what they are saying. But you might inadvertently give them the idea that you are not focused on the interview and that you are thinking about something else entirely.

Ideal posture

As a good interviewer, you should sit up straight in your chair, lean forwards to show attentiveness, and make eye contact with your candidate as often as possible. You may use hand gestures positively to illustrate what you are saying. You will certainly keep your arms and legs unfolded throughout the interview. You may or may not feel the need to smile and reassure, but you should certainly appear to be listening and attentive at all times. Don't forget that to get the best out of a candidate you need to build rapport with them as early in the interview as possible.

The same rules about body language also apply to the candidate sitting in front of you. What signals are his or her posture and body language giving out? Is she relaxed? Does he seem tense or stressed? Is she sitting still, or constantly fidgeting in her chair? In addition to their posture, there are one or two important cases to look out for:

- Nail biting. If the candidate is biting his nails whenever he is not speaking, he is probably someone of a nervous disposition. Make sure you probe this further, and ask questions that might establish their ability to handle pressure.
- Relaxed. If the candidate is leaning right back in his chair, with his arms behind his neck, you might conclude that he is confident and relaxed. However, is this body language appropriate during an interview for a job? You might equally conclude that this posture is inappropriate, or even indicative of an arrogant candidate.
- Looking away. If your candidate looks away before answering a question, it usually means that they are considering quickly the answer they think you want to hear. They may also be fiddling with their hands, or subconsciously doing something distracting like brushing fluff from their jacket or trousers. If you spot this behaviour, you need to ask further questions to ensure that you are hearing what the candidate believes, rather than what they think you want to hear.

Listening skills

Good listening skills are probably the most essential attributes of an interviewer. If a candidate recognizes that you are listening to what they are saying, they are far more likely to open up and keep talking. The poor interviewer will spend as much time asking questions, and telling the candidate about the organization, as they do listening to what the candidate has to say.

Here are some classic examples of poor listening that you should avoid:

- You realize that you are talking as much, or even more, than the interviewee.
- You start to listen to an answer that your candidate gives. After a while, you realize that your mind has wandered, and that you have 'turned off'. There is no chance to follow up what the candidate has said with another question because you do not know what they have said.
- You interrupt a candidate because you have suddenly remembered a question that you meant to ask earlier. You'd better ask it now or else you will forget it again.
- You find yourself repeating a question, albeit phrased in a different way, because you can't remember the answer they gave initially.

There are a number of proven methods for improving your listening skills:

- Summarize what a candidate says to demonstrate that you are listening. Say something like: 'I see. So what you are saying is that you want to find a job where you will be working more within a team. Is that right?'
- Jot down any questions that occur to you during the interview. Find a convenient point to ask them, rather than interrupt what they are saying.
- Sit up straight and adopt an attentive posture. Nod and make other gestures at key points.
- Smile or show concern where appropriate. Your facial expressions will indicate the degree to which you are listening.
- Just listen!

Controlling an interview

No matter how well prepared you are, at some stage you will come up against one of a number of 'problem' candidates who will throw you off course. Here are some of the more common ones, together with suggestions about how to handle them.

Know-all

This is the candidate who appears to know everything about the job and your organization already. They even seem to know what they want to say before you have even asked the question. There is nothing they really need to know, so the only questions they are likely to ask are about why you are appointing for this particular role. They may have one or two alternative ideas to suggest to you. Know-alls tend to be 'big picture' rather than 'detail' people. In other words they are better when discussing general principles rather than facts. So the best way to handle the know-all is to ask a number of specific, probing questions. Request detail. Challenge generalities.

Leaving the tracks

This is the candidate who is unable to stay on course. You ask a question. They begin their answer. Yet within a minute they have somehow managed to change the subject to the football match on television the previous evening. Did you see it? Wasn't it fantastic? As the interviewer, you must retake control. The first time this happens, you might say something like: 'We appear to be drifting off course. Can we return to your customer service experience? How many staff did you supervise?'.

If the candidate digresses repeatedly then it is legitimate to interrupt every time it happens. Start asking a series of closed questions that make changing the subject harder.

Aggressor

It doesn't happen very often, but once in a while you will be faced with an interviewee who is determined to cause trouble. They might argue with you, or challenge what you ask or say. They might accuse you of bias or discrimination. The most important rule is that you must not rise to the bait. Your role is to remain cool and composed throughout the interview. Apart from anything else, the aggressive candidate will want you to argue back, and you will remain in control of the interview if you decline to do so. Close the interview as soon as you can, thank the candidate for expressing their views, and send a polite rejection letter after a couple of days.

The interview psychologist

This is the candidate who tries to find a hidden meaning in every question you ask. Even a simple question might evoke a sly, understanding grin from the candidate, suggesting that he has spotted the hidden depth of what you are asking. You can often spot this character trait because the candidate may try to answer even the simplest question in an unnecessarily complicated way. Bring this to their attention, and ask the question again. If the symptoms reappear periodically, it is probably best to bring the interview to a close, and move on to the next candidate.

Who's interviewing who?

This is the candidate who answers any question that you ask with another question. For example:

'Tell me about your experience managing a team?'
'Why? Surely you aren't looking for a team leader for this role?'

It can be very hard to handle a candidate of this sort, and fortunately they are extremely rare. If you are unfortunate enough to interview such a candidate, you should politely remind them that you are controlling the interview, and that there will be plenty of opportunity to ask questions later. If this fails to address the problem, it is best just to draw the interview to a polite conclusion and move on to the next candidate.

Recording details of an interview

If you are interviewing a number of candidates, it is vital that you have a system for recording or noting what is said, as well as the facts that emerge during the course of the interview. Do not rely on your memory to remember the answers each candidate gives to particular questions.

If you are able to listen while writing notes, then do so. Keep a clean sheet of paper next to the candidate's application or CV, and jot down pertinent facts and answers as the interview progresses. If you need to concentrate on what the candidate is saying, then at least spend the first five minutes after each interview summarizing what was discussed. If you are conducting interviews with a colleague, or as part of a panel, then perhaps one of you should take on the role of note taker. This will free up the rest of the interviewing panel to ask questions and to listen to the answers given.

If the candidate does not object, you might want to consider making a tape recording of the interview. This ensures that you concentrate on listening, rather than making notes. There are two guidelines that you should observe, however:

1 The candidate's permission must be sought.
2 Once a candidate has been rejected, the tape recording must be destroyed.

Your main role must be to listen and observe, so give thought to how best to record what is discussed.

Closing an interview

It may be tempting to rush through an interview if you are certain that you will not be employing the candidate in front of you. However, you should aim to bring any interview to a polite and unhurried conclusion. Remember that every candidate has gone to considerable effort to submit their application, and they deserve to be treated with dignity and respect.

Questions

You need to make sure that you allow time for candidates to ask their own questions. If the candidate has prepared carefully, they should have at least a couple of questions to ask. Inevitably you may feel disappointed if there appears to be nothing that the candidate wants to find out, but bear in mind that you may have already answered the question that they might have asked during the course of the interview. If the candidate appears unwilling to ask a question, you can try to encourage them:

• Is there anything I can tell you about the way the company pension scheme operates?
• Is there anything concerning the job that you are not clear about?

If you believe that the candidate is not asking questions because they are not interested in the vacancy, then now is the time to ask: 'Are you still interested in the position now that you have heard more about it?'

Conclusion

There are several items that you may want to cover at the end of the interview:

- You may wish to tell the candidate how many people you intend to interview, and how many you have interviewed so far.
- Perhaps you should let the candidate know when you plan to conduct second interviews.
- What notice period must the candidate give to their current employer?

When you are certain that you have covered all the necessary details, thank the candidate for their time, shake their hand, and escort them from the building.

Spontaneous offers

It may be tempting to make a spontaneous offer of employment to an excellent interviewee. After all, you have established that they have several interviews with other companies, and if you don't snap them up then someone else will.

In most cases you should hold back. You need time to review the interview, and to make certain that they meet all of your requirements. Just because they interviewed well doesn't mean that they are perfect for the job. Sometimes, however, you should follow your instinct. You should not risk losing an excellent candidate, and so making a provisional offer would be the right thing to do. A provisional offer can be retracted if new information comes to light, but might nevertheless encourage the candidate to decline other offers of employment.

In many organizations there are measures in place that prevent a spontaneous offer of employment. If you work for a smaller organization where no such measures are in place, you should not rule out such a possibility.

Checklist

✓ Is your posture appropriate?
✓ Are you listening attentively?
✓ What is your interviewee's body language telling you?
✓ How would you cope with a candidate who appears to 'know it all'?

✓ How would you keep a digresser on track?
✓ Could you handle an aggressive candidate?
✓ What steps have you taken to record the interview or make notes?
✓ Have you left time for the candidate's questions?
✓ Would you know how to bring an interview to a conclusion?
✓ Should you make a spontaneous offer?

part

five

selecting applicants

selection tests

In this chapter you will learn:

- about the different selection tests you could use
- when to use each type of test
- how to introduce games and role play.

In addition to the interview itself, there are a number of selection methods and tests that you can ask your shortlisted candidates to perform. Which tests work best, and which are appropriate for your vacancy?

For many vacancies, the process of shortlisting candidates from an application form or CV, then conducting one or more interviews, will be sufficient for making an informed appointment. However, it is increasingly common to employ a range of selection tests as part of the recruitment process. Selection tests fit broadly into one of the following categories:

- aptitude tests (testing appropriate skills or knowledge required for the position)
- intelligence tests (commonly known as IQ tests)
- personality tests (attempting to match a candidate's personality traits with those required of the job holder)
- work sample tests (asking the candidate to perform actual or realistic appropriate work tasks)
- cognitive or psychological tests, that are often referred to collectively as psychometric tests.

The skill is to introduce only such selection testing methods that are appropriate for the position for which you are recruiting. It is a good idea when reviewing the job and person specifications to consider how you might establish that a candidate fulfils each requirement. Is there a simple task that you could ask a candidate to perform that would confirm this? For some requirements, it is very simple. For example, you could ask a candidate to type a letter to check for speed and accuracy. But for other circumstances, it is much harder. How would you test that a candidate works well as part of a team, for example?

There are a variety of techniques available to make your recruitment decision more scientific, and less of a gut reaction.

Attainment tests

These test a candidate's basic skills or knowledge and can be as simple as an elementary spelling, grammar or arithmetic test included as part of the first or second interview stage. Other examples include:

- speed typing test (if the vacancy is secretarial)
- financial calculations (if an accounting, book-keeping or management position)
- translation test (if the vacancy requires two or more languages).

An attainment test can provide stark and irrefutable evidence of a candidate's ability. Occasionally, the most impressive person at interview will fail the simplest of arithmetic tests, making them wholly unsuitable for the position. If you decide to use attainment tests, make sure that all candidates complete the same questions in the same conditions. It may sound obvious, but do not allow a favoured candidate to complete their test at home, and send it in at a later stage. The results of the tests are only useful if every candidate is treated in the same way.

It is also risky to assume that the standard of written English on a candidate's CV or application form is a reflection of their communication skills at large. Someone may have helped them with their application, or even written it for them. An attainment test is a quick way to check.

Personality tests

How do you measure a candidate's personality? Surely that is something you gauge when talking to them at interview? You form an opinion about whether the candidate is shy or outgoing, confident or nervous, challenging or submissive. To a degree, this is true. However, a number of personality tests are available that are designed to predict how a candidate is likely to perform in a particular working environment. They range from the simple, quick questionnaire to the complex and sophisticated psychological evaluation.

Personality tests often follow a similar format: candidates must answer a hundred or more multiple-choice questions in a short period of time. The principle is that a candidate must provide an almost instant, instinctive response to each question. There are no right or wrong answers, just personal ones.

In reality, personality tests can only give a broad indication of a candidate's behaviour in a given situation, or provide a means for measuring extremes of personality. For example, a test might highlight that a candidate is confident to the point of arrogance, which would be inappropriate for someone joining a small,

For each of the following pairs of words or statements choose the one that more clearly reflects **how you would prefer to work** and put an (a) or (b) **in the final column.**

Set One – How I prefer to work

	(a)	(b)	(a) or (b)
1	When dealing with complexity I first like peace and quiet so that I can concentrate on the issues	When dealing with complexity I first like to discuss the issues with some of my colleagues	
2	An overview of situations helps me understand what is needed before going into detail	I first seek to understand detail before looking at the wider picture	
3	I like a work environment that is both supportive and harmonious	Using facts to support a logical analysis	
4	One step at a time	Follow my hunches	
5	I like to formulate a plan and then follow it	Holding my options open in case of last-minute changes	
6	Close to deadlines – I'm good at crisis management	Well in advance of when work is due	

Set Two – What interests me at work

	(a)	(b)	(a) or (b)
7	Variety and action	A 'decent' task that I can get my teeth into	
8	Creativity and innovation	Practical application of experience and learned skills	
9	Reaching a decision quickly	Generating lots of options	
10	Finding solutions people will accept and implement	Applying logic to decisions	
11	Mutual respect	People's values	
12	Realistic targets	Outperforming others	

personality test sample extract

established team. The main drawback of personality tests lies in the belief that one is qualified to define the optimum personality required for a given role. It is straightforward to define the skills required in a job or person specification, but much harder to conclude from it the personality traits desired. Nevertheless there are occasions when using a personality test is desirable. Examples include:

- as an initial screening device in order to reject candidates who are obviously unsuited to the role
- when recruiting a new member into an established team or department
- when recruiting for roles demanding a particularly outgoing, confident person.

If you decide to include a personality test as part of your recruitment process, make sure that you:

- get expert and professional help to interpret the results
- balance the test results with other factors, such as how the candidate performed at interview
- do not read too much into the answers given. It is very easy to take one of the answers too literally (e.g. prefer playing squash to playing rugby), and draw an inappropriate conclusion (e.g. this person would not enjoy working as part of a team).

Handwriting tests

Some organizations employ handwriting experts to determine personality characteristics, and so aid the selection process. Handwriting experts, called graphologists, can measure factors such as self-esteem, creativity, energy levels, honesty and ability to work with others. Supporters of handwriting tests claim that they are as reliable a predictor of personality as a number of other more complex personality tests. But remember that the same shortfalls as for other personality tests will apply.

Results from handwriting tests are best used to confirm findings from other tests, and as just one part of the selection process. Always employ the services of an expert when interpreting a candidate's handwriting. Never assume that you are able to do it yourself!

Intelligence tests

A number of sophisticated techniques exist to test a candidate's visual, numerical and verbal reasoning. You may remember having to answer questions that involve identifying a pattern or sequence amongst words or numbers. For example:

$2 - 4 - 8 - 16 - ? - 64 - 128$

Spatial awareness is often tested by having to identify the odd one out in a series of similar shapes. Before incorporating intelligence tests into your selection process, you should consider how important intelligence is for the role. A repetitive manual role would not require a highly intelligent person so, as with all selection methods, make sure that the test you use is appropriate for the role for which you are recruiting.

If the role requires an ability to learn quickly, reason or act decisively, you may wish to use intelligence tests as part of the selection process. Remember, though, that roles requiring high intelligence probably also require common sense, communication skills and interpersonal skills, so make sure that these are given equal priority.

Work sample tests

Ideally, you would like to know how well a shortlisted candidate would perform in the actual job before you appoint them. Although this is rarely possible, you could ask the candidate to perform an actual or simulated task that is typical to the role. Such tasks are called work sample tests, or analogous tests. They are reasonably straightforward to devise, and you can base them on actual events or create a scenario or problem that the job holder is likely to face. The examples below demonstrate how to include a work sample test in a variety of jobs.

Customer service roles

Typically, the role may involve responding to customer requests or complaints by letter. An appropriate test might be to give the candidate an actual or fictitious letter of complaint, and ask them to respond to it. If the role requires good telephone skills, get a colleague to assume the role of a customer, and ask the candidate to phone them.

Accounting roles

Junior accounting roles often involve book-keeping, bank reconciliation or maintaining simple balance sheets. You could give the candidate a sample balance sheet containing errors, and ask them to correct it.

Cashier roles

You would have to give the candidate a few simple instructions first, but why not get them to cash up an actual till? This gives you a very accurate picture of how quickly and efficiently they would perform this task in the role.

Secretarial

There are a variety of work sample tests you could set for secretarial recruits. For example, you could provide handwritten notes from a meeting, and ask the candidate to design and type up the minutes. Or you could mark up some corrections in pen to a previously typed report, and ask the candidate to correct it. In fact, you could create a realistic in-tray of a number of appropriate tasks, giving you the opportunity to see how the candidate prioritizes and sorts their workload, and then how they perform each task.

Sales roles

Selling often involves making presentations to key clients. Why not ask candidates to give a ten-minute presentation as part of the second interview? This may put some candidates off, but that is probably a good thing: it demonstrates that either they are poor presenters, or that they cannot be bothered to spend time preparing for it. Either way, you have identified that they are wrong for the role.

For most roles, it is possible to think up a suitable work sample test to include as part of the selection process. But, as with other testing methods, do not place too much emphasis on the results of a single test. A candidate who has done a similar job before is likely to perform the task much better than someone who is new to the role. But that does not mean that the candidate new to the role could not learn how to perform the task just as well. So you should employ work sample tests to confirm a shortlisted candidate's suitability for the role, rather than simply appoint the person who performs the task best. And don't forget that you are only testing how a candidate performs a task, not how well they work with other people.

Games/role play

There are some testing methods that are best used with a short-listed group of candidates. It might be appropriate to bring together the candidates, and ask them to work collectively on a variety of tasks. If you think that this approach is appropriate for the role you are recruiting for, you will get more from it if you employ a professional team builder or psychologist to work with you. Try to get the candidates together for three or four hours, so that you can try out a number of group tests.

Problem solving

You could present a problem, real or imagined, for the group to solve collectively. Look for the leaders, the followers, the know-alls and the reflective candidates. How quickly do they start working as a team, rather than a collection of individuals? Who is binding this team together?

Role play

The right role play scenario will vary from job to job, but split the candidates into pairs, and provide them with realistic situations to work with. You will notice that some candidates love role play, and others hate it. Some candidates treat it as a big joke, while others take it very seriously.

Discussions

It can be useful to bring the group together around a table, and give them a topic to discuss amongst themselves. You can steer the group to get them started, but then leave the momentum to them. This can be a very stressful scenario for the candidates, so do not expect the conversation to flow straight away. You should not intervene, however, but take a back seat and observe how the group performs. Who is bold enough to start the conversation? Who remains quiet throughout? Who argues strongly?

Social situations

It may be appropriate to end the event with a social gathering with other members of the organization. If the role requires good social skills then this may be particularly appropriate. You can observe who introduces themselves confidently, and who cowers in a corner of the room. Who talks with their mouth full? These things matter!

Checklist

✓ Would a selection test assist your recruitment procedure?
✓ Which selection test would you use?
✓ Is there a suitable work sample test you could devise?
✓ Would a role play exercise fit the culture of your organization?

17

post-interview analysis

In this chapter you will learn:

- how to select candidates for a second interview
- about job previews and other ways to make certain that you have made the right choice.

So the first interviews are over. Now it is time to review all the candidates that you have seen. This is a very important step and one you must take as soon after the first interviews are concluded as possible.

After the interview

If you have conducted several interviews over a short time period then your memory of each of the candidates may be beginning to blur into one another. During the interviews we suggested that you took notes, and one of the reasons for this will now be apparent. At the very least your notes should enable you to distinguish between the various candidates you have interviewed.

If more than one person was involved in the interviewing process it is important that you get together and discuss your findings as a group. You should review each candidate in turn, discuss their strengths and weaknesses, and decide on the next steps to take:

- Do you think that you have interviewed the ideal candidate?
- Will you conduct second interviews?
- Will you need to cast the net wider in order to interview more candidates?

Looking at each candidate in turn, you need to compare and contrast how they performed against the job description and person specification. Which candidate matched all the essential requirements of the role, and most or all of the desirable requirements? Which candidate most closely matched your organization's culture? Which candidates proved unsuitable for the role after interview? If you have used selection tests as part of the interview (see Chapter 16), then which candidates scored highest?

Instinct

As far as possible, you are looking for facts, rather than instinct, to form the basis of your analysis. So look through your notes, and any scoring methods that you used to establish which interviewees performed best.

Instinct, however, can play an important part. You shouldn't ignore it completely. You may have had a gut feeling during the interviewing that one particular candidate would perform best in the role, and would fit in well in your organization. It would be risky to appoint on the basis of a gut feeling alone, but if you are able to support this instinctive reaction with some solid fact and evidence, then you may have identified the right candidate.

Your first choice

The first interview can often reveal a clear 'first choice' candidate to you, although members of an interview panel can often disagree. More common is to have a shortlist of two or three candidates whom you will want to meet again for a second interview. There are a number of steps that you must take:

1 Identify the candidate(s) whom you will want to interview for a second time. You should contact them to arrange a suitable time and location for the second interview.
2 Send a polite rejection letter to candidates whom you interviewed, and who you would not employ for the role, even if your preferred candidate(s) turned the job down. The letter should thank them for their application, and for attending the first interview.
3 You may have a reserve list of candidates. Although they are not in your preferred shortlist for second interviews, you may want to interview them again if your preferred shortlisted candidates turn down the job. You should send these candidates a polite 'stalling' letter, stating that you will get in touch once the initial interviews have been reviewed and analysed.

Second interviews

Second interviews are not always necessary. If you work in a smaller organization, have conducted the interviews alone, and think you have met the right candidate for the position, then why spend more time interviewing them again? It is a personal decision, but you should always remember the costs associated with recruitment. If you get it wrong, you will have to start the recruitment process all over again. So it does no harm to interview your preferred candidate for a second time, just to make certain.

In larger organizations, you may have a number of first interviewees who you want to see again. They will each have different strengths and weaknesses, and the second interview can be used to reveal the best candidate. Your first interview analysis and review should have identified a shortlist of perhaps four or five candidates at most. If you have a longer shortlist than this, then you should probably look back over the first interviews and try to reduce it further.

Second interviews are often mishandled. Many organizations call applicants in for a second time, only to meet the same people who ask the same list of questions. There is little point in conducting second interviews if this is what you plan to do. You should use the second interview to:

• introduce candidates to other members of the management team, or the department that the successful candidate will work with
• ask a different selection or type of questions
• give candidates one or more selection tests (see Chapter 16)
• ask shortlisted candidates to make a presentation
• probe further into a candidate's perceived area of weakness.

You should try to include one or more interviewers who were not involved the first time. They may offer new observations about particular candidates.

Second interview outcomes

The second interview, together with any selection tests you employ, should result in one of three outcomes:

1 You identify your preferred candidate.
2 You decide that none of your shortlisted candidates is suitable.
3 You still have more than one preferred candidate.

Clearly the first outcome is ideal. You should make the candidate an offer of employment, and begin the process of bringing them in to your organization (see Chapter 18). Remember not to reject the other second interviewees until your preferred candidate has accepted your offer, has passed any fitness or medical tests, and you have followed up their references to your satisfaction.

If you find that none of your second interviewees is right for the role, then don't be afraid to admit it. It is more common than you think. Don't be tempted to appoint one of the candidates in any case. Look back at your reserve list, but if no other likely candidates emerge, then it is probably time to re-advertise. You should review the wording that you used in your advertisement to see if you can amend it in a way that will attract more suitable applicants second time around. Some organizations also add the words 'Previous applicants need not apply' to ensure that they do not receive another application from a candidate who they have already rejected.

The third outcome, where you still have two or more preferred candidates after second interview, is trickier. You need to go back to all the evidence that you have available. Score each candidate against the job description, the person specification, the tests, the presentations and the interview performance. All candidates may be able to do the job, but you must be able to identify a winner using all these criteria together.

Making certain

Even if the second interviews have identified one outstanding candidate, you may still feel nervous about committing yourself by making an offer. There are one or two methods you can use to confirm that you have found the right candidate and have made the correct decision. If your preferred candidate is willing, a job preview might be the answer.

Job previews

However well your preferred candidate has performed in tests and in interviews, the greatest test of how suitable he or she is comes when they actually start to do the job itself. Only then will you see how well your new employee:

- copes with the demands of the job
- handles pressure and stress
- gets on with colleagues and staff
- manages the staff they are responsible for
- delivers the performance targets they have been set.

How about if you could see your preferred candidate perform in the role before you confirmed their appointment? Sounds attractive, doesn't it? In theory, offering your preferred candidate a job preview gives both you and the candidate that opportunity:

1   You have the chance to see them perform the role.
2   The candidate gets the chance to see if the role suits them.

In practice, however, there are some pitfalls to avoid, even when trying to organize a simple three-day job preview:

- Can you put together a realistic three days' work that would be part of the selected job holder's actual role? If you can't, or it would be difficult to do so, then it may not be appropriate to offer a job preview. After all, there is not much point in establishing how well your candidate can do work that they will not have to do once they have joined your organization.
- How realistic is it to expect your candidate to commit to a job preview? If they are already employed elsewhere, for example, then it would be unfair to expect them to try to take several days off work to undertake a job preview. Likewise, it would be unrealistic to expect them to leave their current role altogether to take up a speculative job preview for your organization. However, if your preferred candidate is not currently employed, or their circumstances are such that it would not be a problem, then a job preview might suit both of you.

The idea of a realistic job preview is to show the candidate what the job is really like, and to see how they perform in the role. Your candidate may welcome the idea, especially if they are unsure about whether or not the position is right for them. But under no circumstances should you penalize or judge a candidate on the grounds that they are unable to commit to a job preview.

Final check

A job preview is just one way to be as certain as you can be about the decision you have made. Remember that you have already followed a methodical step-by-step process to arrive at your decision:

1 You listed the demands and responsibilities of the role in a job description.
2 You identified the essential and desirable requirements of the ideal candidate in the person specification.
3 You compared and contrasted all the applications you received against these two documents.
4 You shortlisted for interview the candidates who best fitted the requirements.
5 You reviewed and assessed the interview performance of each candidate against these optimum criteria.
6 You may have asked shortlisted candidates to perform one or more practical or behavioural tests.
7 You shortlisted again, and conducted second interviews.
8 You may, or may not, have asked your preferred candidate to undertake a job preview.

Making a decision

You should now be in a position to commit to a decision to make an offer of employment to your preferred candidate. Any doubts you still have might be put down to nerves, or could indicate that none of your shortlist is suitable. Always bear in mind that the perfect candidate almost certainly doesn't exist. Assuming that you have identified your preferred candidate, it is time to make them an offer.

Checklist

✓ Have you reviewed the performance of each candidate as soon as the first interviews are completed?

✓ Has instinct led you to favour one particular interviewee?

✓ Do you have a 'first choice' candidate?

✓ Will you hold second interviews?

✓ How will they be different from the initial interviews? Who else can you involve?

✓ Have the second interviews identified one candidate above all others?

✓ Do you feel ready to make your preferred candidate a job offer?

✓ Have you rejected all of your second interviewees?

✓ Would a job preview be appropriate in your case?

✓ Is it time to make your decision?

18

making the offer and taking up references

In this chapter you will learn:

- how to make verbal and written offers
- how to take up references
- what conditions you should include in your offer of employment.

So you have reached your decision about who to appoint. Now it is time to make them an offer and negotiate terms and conditions. What will you do if they turn your offer down? What if another organization makes a counter offer? If they accept, what conditions should you impose on your job offer? When should you take up references? How should you interpret another employer's reference?

Making a verbal offer

You can save yourself a lot of time by making a job offer verbally in the first instance. Summarize the nature of the job you are offering, as well as the benefits and salary that the position attracts. Give the candidate time to ask any questions they may have, and do not be surprised if they ask for a little time to consider your offer. You may feel a little disappointed that the candidate does not jump at the opportunity to work for your organization. This is natural, but unjustified. Accepting a job is potentially a life-changing decision for anyone, and so you should be delighted that they are considering carefully the offer you have made.

If you are sure that you have interviewed the candidate who you would like to employ, there is nothing to stop you making a verbal, and conditional, offer of employment there and then. However sure you are, though, don't make an offer until you have seen all the interviewees. It is unfair and unethical to interview someone whom you have no intention of employing. If you are unable to make the offer at the end of the interview, then it is perfectly acceptable to telephone the candidate to make your verbal offer. This is a good time to ask permission to approach the candidate's referees for a reference, and make arrangements for a medical, if this is one of the conditions of employment. You should take the opportunity to agree a likely start date.

Think beforehand about what action you will take if your chosen candidate declines your offer. Will you raise your offer, or try to negotiate terms? If there is one candidate who is clearly superior to the rest, this may be your best option. However, you must indicate that you have a line above which you will not cross: you might raise your offer once, but if you are still not close to terms that are acceptable to your chosen candidate, then you are better off moving on to your second choice.

Making a written offer

If your preferred candidate accepts your verbal offer of employment, then you should put this offer in writing at the earliest opportunity. It is very unlikely that a candidate will resign from their current employment without a written job offer from you. So the longer you delay putting your offer in writing, the longer you will have to wait for your new employee to start.

Your written job offer should contain all of the following details:

- Job title
- Job description
- Job location
- Job title and name of superior
- Main terms and conditions
- Salary
  - level
  - payment dates and payment frequency
  - payment method
  - overtime
- Anticipated/realistic working hours
- Breaks
- Holidays and time off
- Benefits that the job attracts (e.g. non-contributory pension; company car)
- Any conditions upon which employment is dependent (e.g. satisfactory references; medical; proof of qualifications)
- Details of probationary period
- Date by which offer should be signed, dated and returned by the new employee, to indicate acceptance of the offer.
- Trial/probationary period
- Start date.

Qualifications

Checking qualifications is an area where you should apply some common sense. There may be some essential qualifications that should be checked first, and thoroughly (e.g. fork lift truck licence; lifeguard qualification; registered childminder). Others may be less important, or even irrelevant. It is generally recognized that people exaggerate or even fabricate certain qualifications, particularly with regard to academic achievement. You must decide which qualifications that your candidate has claimed are important to the position, and to your organization. Check these thoroughly. At the same time, you should not delay your candidate's employment until such time that they can prove that they did, in fact, achieve an award that is not relevant to the position (such as their GCSE Art grade). Naturally, you will want to confirm your preferred candidate's honesty, but you also want them to start their employment as soon as is practical.

Also, when confirming qualifications, start in reverse order with the most recent qualification gained. For example, if you confirm that your candidate did, as they claim, achieve an upper second degree in Modern Languages, why would they lie about their GCSE grades in history or geography? Although schools and colleges are unlikely to give you any background to the candidate's experience, they should be able to confirm grades or awards made, or even provide a duplicate certificate.

Salary

If possible, you should leave the salary negotiation as late as you can. Your rigorous recruitment process has identified your preferred candidate. Now it is time to see whether or not you can afford them! If you spend too long dwelling on salary during the interview process, the danger is that you will be influenced by a candidate who you know you can pay less than you anticipated, or be put off by a candidate who you think will be too demanding.

First of all, you must ensure that the salary you are able to offer is, at least, competitive. To be competitive, you can include benefits of the position other than the actually salary paid. For example, does the position come with a company car? Does your organization offer cheap loans for travel/commuting purposes? Is there a pension scheme that new employees can join? Will the new employee benefit from a performance related bonus? All these extra benefits can be used as bargaining tools when you are discussing remuneration with your chosen candidate. If he or she declines your offer on the grounds of salary, see if you can make the overall package more attractive by offering one or more of these benefits.

Counter bids

Some candidates may use an offer of a new position as a tool to manoeuvre extra benefits or a salary rise from their current employer. If successful, they may then come back to you requesting you to up your offer. It is up to you how you react in this situation. You may take the view that this is not behaviour you expect from someone who is about to represent your organization. Conversely, if the position you are trying to fill requires someone with confidence and determination, you may applaud this action and submit to your candidate's demands. A similar scenario might arise if a candidate has two job offers from which to choose. This is a perfect opportunity for the candidate to secure the best deal they can before accepting either offer of employment. Ultimately, the culture of your organization will determine how to react to counter bids of this sort.

Notice periods

If the candidate you want to employ already has a job with another organization, they will almost certainly be required to serve a notice period. This will vary between organizations, but will normally be at least one calendar month. However impatient you may feel about wanting to bring your preferred candidate on board quickly, do not apply pressure to encourage them to leave their current employment early. It is unprofessional, and you would probably not want the same treatment to be applied to one of your employees.

For senior positions, you can expect the notice period to be longer. Often, people in management positions might have to serve three months' notice, and company directors may be locked in to a notice period of six months. Whilst these are not always enforced, you should assume that they will be until you hear otherwise.

So as someone who wants to recruit your new member of staff quickly, what steps can you take? To begin with, you need to assess the level and type of position you are recruiting. If you are recruiting for a low-skilled position, you might take notice periods into account. If you have a shortlist of two adequately qualified candidates, and one can start straight away, then you might legitimately choose this candidate ahead of the other one. For senior or skilled positions, this is counterproductive. You should always appoint on the basis of the person most skilled, qualified and suitable for the position. The length of time that you must wait to employ them is a secondary consideration.

Although an employee may be contracted to serve three months' notice for their current employer, they may be asked to leave the moment they resign. Many organizations take the view that there is a security issue by continuing to employ someone who is about to leave, particularly if they plan to join a competitor organization. So you might find that you resolve to wait three months for your new member of staff, only to find that they can start work immediately. You never can tell.

Taking up references

All offers of work should be made subject to the receipt of satisfactory references. In the initial application, or after interview, it is common to ask candidates for the names of two or more referees. These might be:

- personal referees, who will provide a character reference
- educational referees, who will confirm qualifications gained or courses studied
- current and former employees, who will have direct experience of working with the candidate.

In practice, the value of these referees is questionable, because the candidate will select the colleagues and former employers who are likely to speak favourably about them. Nevertheless, you must follow up references before confirming any offer of work that you make, and you should try to get as much supporting evidence as you can from the referees that you have.

Former and current employers

The former or current employer is likely to be the most useful reference to you, so it is a good idea to contact them first. You must only contact a referee with permission from the candidate, and you should not assume the worst if they are reluctant to allow you to contact their current employer. There are a number of legitimate reasons why this would create a problem for the candidate, and you should respect this.

Remember the situation. You have made a job offer subject to the receipt of satisfactory references. The candidate may wish to leave their current employer because of a personality clash, or even harassment. The current employer is likely to give a poor reference, leading you to decline to employ the candidate. The candidate now has to continue working with an even more difficult employer who knows that the candidate is trying to leave. So you must respect a candidate's individual circumstances, and settle for a former employer. You can always contact the current employer after the job offer is confirmed, to verify basic facts about the candidate's role.

Whenever you take up references, you are looking for evidence to support your belief that this candidate is right for the role you wish to offer them. You should take the opportunity to:

- verify facts about previous work experience
- confirm opinions you have made about the candidate
- re-evaluate a candidate in the light of what you have learned.

Making contact

Although you should write to a referee in the first instance, you will get more out of the reference if you contact the referee by telephone. Referees tend to be guarded about what they will commit to in a letter. They will not want the candidate to see negative comments about them on paper, especially as this could lead to legal action if the comments are defamatory. On the telephone, referees tend to be more open and realistic when discussing a candidate, although bear in mind that they will still be careful about what they say.

As with an interview, plan what you want to ask the referee before you pick up the telephone. You will get much more out of the referee if you ask specific questions rather than request a general endorsement of the candidate. Examples include:

- factual questions, such as the dates that the candidate was employed, the position that they held, or the salary that they earned

- details of the responsibilities that the candidate held, including the number of staff in their charge and their management status
- emotive questions such as why the candidate is leaving.

You may find that the referee is evasive when answering certain questions. Employment and discrimination laws are notoriously tough, and the referee may simply be protecting him/herself legally. In fact, some organizations have a policy of confirming only that an employee was employed by them.

If you want to take up reference by letter, there is little value in writing to the referee asking for a general reference about the candidate. You are much better off thinking through and noting carefully all the questions that you would like answered about the candidate and state them carefully within the wording of the letter. You may wish to include a questionnaire addressing some or all of the following issues:

- position held
- dates employed
- responsibilities
- daily tasks
- attendance and timekeeping record
- behaviour/conduct
- performance
- honesty and integrity
- health
- reason for leaving
- would you re-employ?

You may wish to send a copy of the job description and person specification to the referee and ask them if they think the candidate is suitable for this particular role. You may not always receive answers to all the questions that you ask, but by preparing thoroughly you stand a good chance of getting back something more useful than a broad endorsement of the candidate's work record.

Tip
Always include a reply-paid envelope with any request for a reference.

Denzil's Stationery

Dear Mr Cross

Your name has been put forward as a referee by James Fothergill,
who has applied for the position of Buyer within our company.

We would be grateful if you could answer the questions below:

What position did he hold in your company?
For how long did he work in this position?
What were the main responsibilities of this position?

Please comment on his:
Time keeping
Conduct
Performance
Health
Honesty
Ability

Please be assured that any information you give will be treated in the
strictest confidence. If you prefer to discuss the matter with me over
the telephone, please call me on (020) 7544 8401.

Thank you for your help in this matter.

Yours sincerely

Alan Denzil

sample reference request letter

Breakspeare Removals Ltd
Reference Request

Applicant's Name: _____

Position Applied For: _____

Role & Responsibilities: _____
_____

We would be grateful if you would give us your assessment of the above named person's ability by completing the questionnaire below:

Teamwork	1	2	3	4	5
Working alone	1	2	3	4	5
People skills	1	2	3	4	5
Work quality	1	2	3	4	5
Work quantity	1	2	3	4	5
Management skills	1	2	3	4	5
Health record	1	2	3	4	5
Attendance record	1	2	3	4	5

Key:
1 = Excellent
2 = Very good
3 = Satisfactory
4 = Poor
5 = Very poor

Would you re-employ this person?
Yes/No

If you would like to add any additional information, please do so here: _____
_____

Your name:
Position:
Date:
Signature:

sample reference request questionnaire

Suspicious references

Although it is unlikely that a candidate will put forward a referee
who will give a bad reference, there are any number of reasons
why this might happen. Some employers believe that the best way
to keep a good candidate is by giving them a poor reference for
any job that they apply for. If there has been any question of discrimination, harassment, or just a personality clash, a current
employer might choose to criticize the candidate's work record
as a means of disguising the real reason.

You should be equally wary of an exemplary reference. Although
illegal, an employer may give a first-class reference for an
employee that they are desperate to lose.

Non-committal references will also need to be interpreted. A reference may say very little for several reasons:

- It may be the organization's policy only to confirm the dates
  between which a candidate was employed.
- The referee may prefer to make a negative comment about a
  candidate, but chooses to avoid this simply by not comment-
  ing on a particular aspect at all.
- They may simply have forgotten to answer a particular question.

You are unlikely to get all the supporting evidence that you
would like from the referees you have been given. The following
checklist will help you get the most out of them:

- be specific in what you ask
- be open and direct when talking to a referee on the telephone
- plan what you want to ask before you write or telephone
- use questionnaires to be even more specific
- try to verify specific facts that the candidate has given you.

Testimonials

It is increasingly common for candidates to support their application with an open letter from a former employer, such as the
one illustrated opposite. Such letters are called testimonials, and
are often issued as part of a redundancy package, or when an
organization is closed down or relocated. You should only regard
a testimonial as confirmation of a candidate's former employment
and the reason that the candidate left. You should be sceptical of
any positive endorsement of the candidate, as such letters are
often produced to a standard format for a number of candidates.

Sydenham Packaging Ltd
39–41 High Road
Sydenham
Kent DA8 7RR

To whom it may concern:

Alex Menhams was employed by me at Sydenham Packaging Ltd between August 1998 and March 2003.

During the time Alex was with us, he worked tirelessly as a valued member of our sales team. He won the Salesperson of the Month award no fewer than six times, and was eventually appointed Sales Manager in June 2001.

I would recommend Alex for a sales role in any organization. He is determined, hard working and energetic.

Jim Swaffer
Managing Director

Checklist

✓ Have you made a verbal offer of employment?
✓ Have you followed this up with a written offer?
✓ Have you checked your preferred candidate's qualifications?
✓ Have you negotiated a mutually acceptable salary?
✓ Have you dealt with any counter bids?
✓ Have you agreed a start date?
✓ Have you taken up references?
✓ Are the references you have received satisfactory?

19

rejecting unsuccessful candidates

In this chapter you will learn:

- how to reject unsuccessful candidates
- how to deal with challenges.

At various stages throughout the recruitment process you will need to write to unsuccessful candidates to reject them. You should reject all but your interview shortlist as soon as you can, but you could defer rejecting your final shortlist until your preferred candidate has accepted your offer of employment. So how should you reject a candidate? What reasons should you give? What should you never say?

Rejecting as you go

It's a very sad fact that many organizations just don't bother to let candidates know if their application has been unsuccessful. This is unprofessional, and displays extremely bad manners. Remember that candidates may have put a great deal of time and effort into their application and it is only proper that you should go to the trouble to both acknowledge and, if necessary, reject unsuitable applications.

If you receive hundreds of applications, your acknowledgement letter could include a sentence such as: 'Shortlisted candidates will be invited to interview on or before 14 March. Applicants who have not been invited to interview may assume that their application has been unsuccessful'. This inclusion in the original acknowledgement letter means that you do not have to send rejection letters to every single applicant, only those who you have shortlisted. You could even include a phrase in the recruitment advertisement such as 'Shortlisted candidates will be notified in writing on or before 14 March'. This then gives candidates a realistic idea about how their application is progressing. If 14 March passes, then they can turn their attention to another application.

Rejecting unsuitable candidates can be a time-consuming and costly process. Despite the cost, it is always worth the effort. Applicants who have not heard from you might contact you direct, to establish the status of their application. This only adds to the administrative burden of the recruitment process. If you send out rejection letters promptly, you will not have to handle these calls. Candidates who have not heard from you are also likely to take offence. After all, they have gone to the trouble of completing your application form, and you have not even bothered to tell them how their application is progressing. Not only are these applicants likely to be offended, they are also likely to tell others about their bad experience with your organization. So it is just not worth failing to take this simple step.

Once you shortlist a candidate, you must treat them differently. You have raised their expectation, and you must treat them courteously if you decide not to offer them employment with you. Although it is never pleasant to receive a rejection letter, it is always better than to hear nothing at all.

Rules for rejection

There are several rules to follow when rejecting candidates.

Be prompt

Once you have received your applications for the vacancy, the first step is to filter out the unsuitable candidates. You should reject these straight away. If they are not right for the position, there is no point in delaying writing a polite letter of rejection. This will help the candidate, as well as you. It will then leave you to concentrate on the applications that are most suitable for the position on offer.

Of course, there will be some applications that you will want to keep hold of in case your preferred candidate turns down your offer of employment. It is perfectly legitimate to choose not to reject these candidates until your preferred candidate has accepted the position in writing. Nevertheless, as soon as your offer has been accepted, you must send a polite rejection letter to all other candidates as soon as possible. In fact, if you retain an application in case your preferred candidate declines your offer, you should let the reserve candidate know the position he or she is in. Tell it to them straight. They will be grateful that they are being kept informed of their progress. Whilst you might want them to think that they were always your number one choice, it is perfectly acceptable to keep a reserve candidate in the wings. Any reserve candidates should be kept regularly informed about any progress. You might also wish to advise any reserve candidates that they should accept alternative employment if they are offered it.

Be brief

It is tempting when rejecting candidates to offer a number of reasons why you have declined to offer them employment. After all, you might feel you are helping them to find a job in the future. Be careful. You are much more likely to get comeback if you offer reasons why you have declined to take an application further.

Even though you are acting in good faith, candidates can challenge the reasons that you give, and take you to an industrial tribunal on discrimination grounds. Indeed, some rejected candidates may contact you to disagree with your reasons for rejection and to try to convince you to change your mind. It is much more common for rejection letters to be quite short, with little or no reason given for the rejection. An example of a rejection letter is illustrated below.

[Current Date]

Dear *[Salutation]*,

I am writing to you regarding your recent application for the position of *[Job Title]* with *[Company Name]*.

We received an excellent response to our advertisement and unfortunately we will not be taking your application any further on this occasion.

I would like to take this opportunity to wish you every success in your future career.
Thank you for your interest in *[Company Name]*.

Your sincerely

[First Name] [Surname]
[Job Title]

As well as being prompt and brief, a good rejection will always be in writing. It might be tempting to reject candidates by telephone. However, this is rarely the right procedure. A rejected candidate might ask questions about precisely why they were rejected, and what they might do in the future to increase their likelihood of being offered an interview. If they are not happy with your answer, they may try to engage you in debate about their suitability for the role. By contrast, if you reject unsuitable candidates in writing, there is far less likelihood that they will contact you to argue about the decision you have made.

To avoid accusations of discrimination, you must keep the details of rejected applicants on file for at least three months. This is the period in which a rejected applicant could complain of unlawful discrimination at an industrial tribunal. If the applications that you are keeping on file include notes about the reasons why you rejected them, then so much the better.

Dealing with challenges

How would you react if one of the rejected candidates contacted you to challenge your decision? It is highly unlikely to happen, but you should know what to do if the situation arises.

Rejected candidates often want to know why they were unsuccessful. Just as with your rejection letter, you should be careful about precisely what you say to an unsuccessful candidate. You should use an unambiguous statement like: we appointed someone who matched our requirements more closely. Sometimes an applicant may ask how this person was more closely matched? In this instance, you do not have to go into any further detail. You should use a sentence like: I am afraid that I am unable to discuss another candidate's application. All applications are treated in confidence.

Whatever you say, there are certain phrases that you should not use under any circumstances. For example, never tell an unsuccessful candidate that he or she is overqualified. This phrase is too often used to indicate that you have appointed someone younger. Even if this is not true, the rejected candidate may assume as much. Never tell a candidate that he or she would not fit in. This may be true, but could be construed as racial, religious, age or gender discrimination. And never lie to a candidate and tell them that you have decided not to appoint any of the applicants to the position, or that you have decided to recruit someone at a different level. This is unprofessional, and extremely rude.

Checklist

✓ When should you reject unsuccessful candidates?
✓ What should you write in a rejection letter?
✓ How would you handle a candidate challenging your decision?
✓ How would you protect yourself against a charge of discrimination?

part six

new employees

20

legal requirements

In this chapter you will learn:

- about the types of contract you might offer
- about the minimum legal requirements regarding employment contracts.

There are all sorts of legal requirements associated with employing staff nowadays. What is a 'written statement'? When should you issue one to your new member of staff? What other legal obligations must you fulfil? What types of contract are there? What type of contract of employment is right for you?

Employment contracts

Whether in writing or not, it is important to understand that a new employee has an implied contract of employment as soon as he or she accepts your offer of employment. There are two implications of this:

1 You must make clear in any job offer that you make, that it is dependent upon the receipt of acceptable references. You should also use the offer of employment letter to state any other conditions on which the offer is dependent.
2 You should issue a written contract of employment as soon as is realistically possible after your new employee has started work.

Under the Employment Rights Act 1996, you have a legal obligation, as an employer, to provide every employee, whether full-time or part-time, with a 'written statement' covering the main terms and conditions relating to the employment. You must issue this statement within the employee's first two months of employment.

As a minimum, these are the features that should appear in any written statement of employment:

• The names of both the employer and the employee.
• The date when the employment commenced.
• The employee's rate of pay and the frequency of wages or salary.
• Information relating to working hours, including start and finish times, shift patterns, breaks, time off, overtime and overtime payments.
• Holiday entitlement, including bank holidays, public holidays and holiday pay.
• The employee's job title, as well as a brief description of the work for which the person was employed.
• The employee's work location.

However, in addition to this legal requirement, it is good practice to protect both the employer and employee by providing a full written contract of employment. So you should include the following details in a written job contract, or provide them separately in other documents, as well as the basic terms and conditions required by law:

- Terms, conditions and benefits relating to sickness or injury, including provision for sickness pay and medical insurance.
- Terms and conditions relating to pensions and pension schemes.
- The employee's notice period that he or she is obliged to give, and entitled to receive, if the contract of employment is terminated.
- Information relating to discipline, dress code, or any other behaviour that is relevant to the work of the employee.
- If the position is short-term, you should also indicate the intended length of employment, or the date when the employment will end.

By law, every contract of employment includes certain contractual terms, whether they are written down or not. For example, employers must adhere to certain working practices, and take appropriate health and safety action. You must provide appropriate health and safety training. You must not take action that may undermine the relationship of trust and confidence with your employees.

In turn, employees must serve their employer honestly and faithfully. They cannot compete with the employer's business, nor may they divulge confidential information. They must work with due diligence, skill and care.

There are also certain statutory rights that all employees are entitled to. These include a minimum period of notice, rights under anti-discrimination laws, the right to choose whether or not to join a particular trade union, and rights under legislation relating to working time and pay. Any attempt by the employer to impose contractual terms that override any of these rights are likely to be unenforceable.

However comprehensive the contract that you draw up, there are other regulations over which you have little control. These include:

Working hours

There is new legislation regarding the maximum number of hours that you can expect an employee to work within a week. There are also laws regarding rest periods, meal breaks and paid holidays. You should seek further advice about these if you have any concerns.

Annual holiday

Employees are entitled to a minimum of four weeks' paid leave each year.

Intellectual property

Usually the employer owns the rights to any intellectual property created by the employee in the course of his or her employment.

Confidentiality

If your employee is likely to be entrusted with confidential information, you should include a confidentiality clause within your written contract. There is an implied duty for employees not to divulge trade secrets, both whilst they are employed by you and after employment has ended. If there are specific areas of confidentiality that concern you, you may wish to set these out within the written contract.

Competition

In reality, it is very hard to stop a former employee from setting up in business to compete with you. You should include a restriction within the contract, but this is only likely to be enforceable for a specified period, and will probably only cover a specified geographical area.

The Employments Act 2002

This new Act requires that all employers include, as a contractual term, any disciplinary and grievance procedures. As an employer, you must ensure that basic terms regarding dismissal, discipline and grievance are incorporated within the terms and conditions of employment. The Act applies to all employees and all grievances, no matter how small. Failure to abide by the statutory minimum will be regarded as a breach of contract, and might therefore result in an employer being taken to court for constructive wrongful dismissal. Whilst it is believed that most employers will already satisfy the requirements of the Act, you must review your contracts of employment to make sure that you do abide by these new regulations.

Non-contractual terms

If there are perks or benefits that accompany a job, you may wish to make it clear if you intend them to be non-contractual. Non-contractual benefits are easier to change or even withdraw altogether. Examples might include health insurance, sales bonuses and certain dress codes. If these are included in the main employment contract, they might lose their status as 'perks', and become forever linked to the job. You may then find it difficult, or even impossible, to review or change any of these benefits in the future.

Types of contract

It is unlikely that you will be able to use a single contract of employment that will cover all employees. You should remember that there are a number of different kinds of employee, each of whom will have particular requirements detailed within the contract. For example:

• full-time employees
• fixed-term contracts
• home workers
• job sharers
• part-time employees
• casual workers.

One way to ensure that the issue of job contracts remains manageable is to provide all employees with a standard written statement (the legal requirement), and then supplement this with specific terms and conditions, relevant to each type of employee, laid out in a separate employment contract.

Employment contract procedure

Ideally, once satisfactory references have been received, you should send out the contract of employment to the candidate along with an unconditional offer of employment. You should ask the candidate to sign a copy of the contract and return it as evidence of their acceptance of its terms.

> **Tip**
> The phrase 'contract of employment' is a little misleading. It need not be a single document. You may wish to refer to the offer letter, the written statement of terms and conditions, a staff handbook, health and safety documents, and any other documents or manuals that together outline what is expected of employer and employee.

Dress code

It can be quite difficult to set out within a contract of employment rules and regulations regarding dress codes and standards. After all, there is a narrow line between what is and what is not acceptable. Often this is a subjective matter. Certainly, if a uniform is required as part of the role, you should indicate this within the contract of employment. In March 2003, an administrative worker at a job centre won a legal case regarding his right not to wear a tie to work. He argued that whilst the male workers were required to wear a shirt and tie, the female workers had no equivalent clothing requirement. Indeed, the female workers were allowed to wear T-shirts. So think carefully before trying to impose dress codes as part of the contract of employment.

Checklist

✓ Have you issued your new recruit with an employment contract?
✓ Do you know what elements should be included in an employment contract?
✓ Have you included terms relating to working hours, annual leave and confidentiality?

21

the first week

In this chapter you will learn:

- what your new employee should know before they start
- how to introduce them effectively into the organization
- how to organize an induction programme.

Your new employee has accepted your offer, and agreed to your conditions of employment. They have served notice with their current employer and have turned up for their first day's work with your organization. What preparation should you have made? How should you use your new recruit's first days with you? What ground do you need to cover? How can you introduce your new recruit effectively into your organization?

Medicals

You may have made the satisfactory performance in a medical examination a condition of an offer of employment. After all, you would not want your new employee to be off sick regularly. You have probably formed an accurate view of your new employee's state of health on the basis of their application and references. However, a medical examination may bring something to light that even your candidate was not aware of. Medicals are particularly important for jobs that require a degree of stamina or fitness.

The medical should take place before your new employee has started to work for you. Both the medical, and the taking up of references, should be complete well in advance of the start date you have agreed with your candidate. If yours is a larger organization, you may have your own medical team who will perform the examination. If you do not have such facilities then private healthcare organizations such as PPP or BUPA could perform them on your behalf. Alternatively, you could ask the candidate to arrange a medical checkup by his or her own doctor. Naturally you should cover any cost involved.

Welcome pack

You might choose to send a welcome pack to the successful candidate at the same time as the offer letter. A welcome pack might contain some, or all, of the following items:

- terms and conditions of employment
- staff handbook or manual
- letter of introduction from Managing Director
- copy of health and safety policy
- details of where and when to arrive on the first day
- copies of organization's brochure or catalogues

- details of pension and health schemes
- what to bring in on first day.

The aim of a well-thought-out welcome pack is to excite the new recruit, to handle any administrative matters and to ensure that he or she is ready for the first day's employment.

The first day

Think about it. Can you remember your first day in a new job? Daunting, wasn't it? As the employer, you have a duty to make the first day run as smoothly as possible, and to make your new recruit feel welcome. So what can you do to prepare for the first day?

A good induction programme (see opposite) will include sensible provision for what the new recruit should cover, whom they should meet and what they should do on their first day. Regardless of what is outlined in the induction programme, there are one or two steps that you can take that will indicate that the new recruit is both expected and welcome:

- Let the person at reception know that the new recruit is expected. Have any identity cards or badges ready for their arrival (if appropriate).
- Have a desk and chair ready, together with any stationery or other requirements. It's remarkable how many organizations leave this until after the new recruit has arrived.
- Try not to cover too much ground on day one.
- It sounds obvious, but make sure that you are actually in the office on your new recruit's first day.
- Have any administrative forms handy and ready for completion by the new recruit. Getting the administration out of the way makes a good use of the first day.
- Take time to catch up at the end of the day. How did your recruit feel the day went? Do they have any questions? Is there any feedback you can give them?

Staff handbook

Every organization will have its own idea about whether to issue a staff handbook and what it should contain. A comprehensive staff handbook could include rules and regulations, company benefits (pensions, healthcare, etc.), the mission statement, extracts from the business plan, quotes from employees about what it is like to work for the organization and so on.

If you have chosen to issue all employees with a comprehensive staff handbook, it ought to include a detailed section on training and development.

The following might help when considering the training and development elements to be included:

Organizational framework
Objectives
Mission statement
Business plan

Individual employees
Principle of fitting in with objectives
Induction policy
Job description policy
Appraisal policy
Who is responsible for training and development
Training and development opportunities
Equal opportunities policy

Induction

What is it?

An induction programme is the process of introducing new employees into their jobs, and into the organization, as quickly and effectively as possible. A well-structured induction programme makes new employees feel welcome, and encourages them to identify with the organization. Induction training of one sort or another takes place in every organization. After all, you show someone new where the kettle is, and make sure they know what time to arrive in the morning!

Increasingly, however, a detailed plan is set out covering what a new employee needs to know, what training and development he or she needs to do the job, who is responsible for teaching them, and over what timescale. Over a period covering the first few weeks in the organization, a new employee will be introduced to the company, its staff and its structure. Administrative details, conditions of employment and rules and regulations will be covered. The new employee will meet the team or department he or she will work in, and will be introduced to each aspect of the new job. The best induction programmes are written and laid out as a checklist, showing clearly who is responsible for each element of training, with space for the new employee to sign when each element has been covered satisfactorily. This way the new employee can see progression through the programme, and the manager responsible for training can monitor the progress made.

Try to strike a balance between formal and informal induction. The process becomes a bureaucratic farce if new employees have to sign a form to confirm that they know where tea bags are stored! The full induction programme checklist will vary from company to company, and from person to person. The following checklist is by no means exhaustive, but you might find it useful when planning your first induction programme.

Induction programme checklist

Introduction

Welcome to company
Explanation of induction programme
Organizational chart

Administration

P45
National Insurance number
Bank details
Brief introduction to accounts department
Complete staff record form
Complete season ticket loan form
Birth certificate/education certificates (if applicable)

Conditions of employment

Working hours (lunch hours, flexitime, overtime, bonuses, etc.)
Salary (when paid, how paid, how often reviewed)
Sickness/Other absence (who to notify, doctor's certificate, statutory sick pay, etc.)
Holiday (no. of days, who to notify, notice required, timing, bank holidays, carrying over holiday, etc.)
Notice period required
Disciplinary procedure
Union representation

Company

History (part of a group, when founded)
Finance (turnover, profitability, growth pattern)
Structure (no. of employees, management structure)
Markets (customers, competitors, products, services)
Organizational objectives (mission statement, business plan)

Building and departments

Tour of building (canteen, coffee machine, toilets, photocopier, fax, e-mail, fire exits, notice boards, etc.)
Sales and Marketing department (structure, introduction to staff, function, objectives, etc.)
Customer Services department (structure, introduction to staff, function, objectives, etc.)
Other departments (structure, introduction to staff, function, objectives, etc.)

Rules and regulations

Smoking
Confidentiality
Security
Petty cash
Expenses

Health and safety

Fire procedure
First aid
Protective clothing
Reporting accidents
Food and drink

Policy awareness

Equal opportunities policy
Race and gender discrimination policy
Maternity leave
Unpaid/compassionate leave
Alcohol and drugs
Discipline and grievance
Use of telephones (how to use them, how to answer them, personal phone calls)
Appearance and attitude
Addressing colleagues and superiors
Internet usage policy

Company benefits

Pension scheme (who qualifies, how to apply, brief outline, company contributions, etc.)
Health insurance (who qualifies, how to apply, brief outline, company contributions, etc.)
Company discounts
Clubs, societies and facilities
Share options
Company car/fuel allowance
Mortgage subsidy
Uniform/clothing allowance

The job

Introduction to department
Introduction to line manager
Function of department
Job description
How job fits into organizational objectives

Training

Training and development policy
Skills gaps identified
Appraisal policy and process

An extract from a sample induction programme is laid out below.

Induction Programme for Marketing Co-ordinator

MONDAY 5 MAY

9 a.m.
Report to reception. To be met by David Carr, Marketing Manager, for initial introductions and a tour of the building.
10 a.m.
Meeting with the Marketing Team to meet Sarah Smith, Deputy Manager; Terry Jacob, Special Projects Manager; and George Koumi, Adminstrator. (Marketing Department Meeting Room)
11 a.m.
Meeting with Alex Pankhurst, Chief Executive. (AP's Office)
11.30 a.m.
Meeting with the Sales Team to meet David Todd, Sales Manager, Jane Howden, Sales Co-ordinator, and Andrew Harris, Lisa Nnando and Nancy Hill, Customer Service Assistants. (Sales Meeting Room)

1. p.m.
Lunch with David Carr and Sarah Smith. (Meet in Reception)
2.30–5 p.m.
IT Training with Philip Kerr. An introduction to the company's Intranet and sales database. (IT Training Room)

TUESDAY 6 MAY

9 a.m.
Presentation by Terry Jacob on the Marketing Department's Special Projects. (Boardroom)
11 a.m.
Meeting with Jane Davies, Accountant, to confirm pay and tax details. (Accounts Department)
12 p.m.
Lunch with David Todd, Sales Manager. (Meet in Reception)
2–5 p.m.
Time in the Marketing Department.

WEDNESDAY 7 MAY

9 a.m.
Seminar by Simon Hunter, Production Department Manager. (Marketing Meeting Room)
11 a.m.
Meeting with John Rowe, Office Manager. (JR's Desk)
1 p.m.
Lunch with Barbara Jones, external Marketing Consultant heading the 'Road Promotion' Campaign. (Meet in Reception)
2 p.m.
Afternoon shadowing Sarah Smith. (SS's Office)

THURSDAY 8 MAY

9 a.m.
Meeting with Catherine Chapman, Deputy Manager HR Department, to explain the Health and Safety Rules and Company's commitment to IIP. (HR Department)
10 a.m.
Meeting with Anne Taylor, Training Manager, to explain training opportunities and to tour the Training Library. (Training Library)
12 p.m.
Lunch with Simon Hunter, Production Department Manager. (Meet in Reception)
2 p.m.
Time in the Marketing Department.

FRIDAY 9 MAY

9 a.m.
Time in the Marketing Department.
12 p.m.
Lunch with David Carr – induction debrief. (Meet in Reception)
2–5 p.m.
Visit to Harman Street Building. Tour by David Trump, Production
Deputy Manager. (Harman Street Reception)

Hints and tips for induction

- Plan an induction programme for each employee in advance.
  Use a general induction programme template if you have one,
  but tailor it to suit each new employee.
- Begin the induction programme with the letter that confirms
  the job offer: explain when to arrive, who to report to, what
  to wear, etc.
- Be realistic about what someone might reasonably take in each
  day. Fill the first day only with things that are absolutely necessary, for example, introduction to immediate colleagues only,
  smoking policy, etc.
- Build a new employee's confidence by giving him/her a small
  task on the very first day that will form part of their role.
- Offer a variety of ways of getting information across.
  Introduce some people as a team, others as individuals, go out
  to lunch with immediate colleagues, and so on. There is a lot
  of information to pick up, and a lot of faces to learn. Variety
  will make this easier.
- New recruits often learn more by shadowing other members
  of staff. They find it interesting, too.
- If you have a company handbook, don't assume that the new
  employee will have read and understood it. Go through it page
  by page if necessary.
- Make anyone new feel welcome by ensuring that they have a
  desk, stationery and a telephone ready when they arrive. This
  is absolutely essential!
- When putting the induction programme together, always consider who would be the most appropriate person to deliver
  each element of training.
- Involve the Managing Director if you can (it makes a good and
  lasting impression) but not if there is a strong chance he or she
  will pull out at the last moment.
- Assigning a mentor to a new employee can be very worthwhile

(this is someone who takes responsibility for the new recruit's welfare throughout the induction programme).

- Use the latter stages of the induction programme to go through the new employee's job description slowly and methodically. Ensure that he or she understands each section of it, and appreciates that it will form the basis of the appraisal at a later date.
- Give new employees a plan of the offices, with the names of the people in each room. Mark on the plan other useful features such as the toilets and kitchen. New employees feel very uncomfortable if they do not know their way around.
- Make sure that you send a memo around before a new employee starts. Tell everyone who is starting, when they start, what job they will do and, perhaps, what their background is. This will ensure that the new employee is welcomed on their very first day.

Benefits of an Induction Programme

A well-planned induction programme for your newly appointed employee will provide many benefits:

- New staff will become effective employees over a much shorter period.
- There will be more staff motivation, and less staff turnover.
- New staff will understand their role within the organization, and what is expected of them.
- They will feel part of their department/team from the beginning.
- They will believe they are making a useful contribution towards the organization's objectives and goals.

Case study
One company with which we are familiar tries to ensure that new employees do virtually nothing that will form part of their main role for the whole of their first week in the company.

New employees spend periods of one or two hours in each department, meeting each member of the team, and learning what they all do. One person acts as mentor throughout the first week, ensuring that the new employee is looked after, and also that he or she learns all the general company rules and regulations. A day out with one of the sales representatives is on the agenda, as well as a stint answering the phones (no matter how senior the new recruit is).

By the end of the first week, the new employee has a very firm grasp of how the organization works, and can begin in week two to learn about the specific role that he or she has been recruited for.

Checklist

✓ Are you fully prepared for your new recruit's arrival?
✓ Have you prepared a desk or place for them to work?
✓ Have you devised a manageable first day?
✓ Do you have an induction programme in place?

appendix: discrimination

You have a duty at all times to ensure that your recruitment procedures are fair, legal and anti-discriminatory.

There are four main areas of discrimination covered by legislation: equal pay; sexual discrimination; racial discrimination; disability. You need to be particularly careful not to discriminate in your recruitment procedures, especially when placing job advertisements. There is a wealth of legislation protecting employers and employees, and in almost all cases it is preferable to take professional legal advice when recruiting, rather than take a risk.

We list below the main acts concerned with discrimination, along with sources where you can get more detailed help and guidance.

Equal Pay Act 1970

The Equal Pay Act (1970) makes it unlawful for employers to discriminate between men and women in terms of their contracts of employment. You need to be aware that it covers all the contractual benefits, not just pay. So there must be equality in relation to:

- holiday entitlement
- pension
- childcare benefits
- sickness benefits
- car and travel allowances.

There are two excellent sources of further information:

- Equal Opportunities Commission www.eoc.org.uk
  They publish a Code of Practice on Equal Pay which gives practical advice and guidance on discrimination, as well as case studies illustrating examples of discrimination on the basis of equality.
- Equality Direct www.equalitydirect.org.uk
  A free service affiliated to ACAS that gives business managers easy access to authoritative advice on a wide range of equality issues. The website has sensible advice and guidance written in plain English, whilst further advice is available for the price of a local phone call.

Sex Discrimination Act 1975

The Sex Discrimination Act makes it unlawful for an employer to discriminate because of a person's sex or marital status when recruiting. Every part of the recruitment process is covered by the Act including:

- job descriptions
- person specifications
- recruitment advertisements
- application forms
- shortlisting procedures
- interviews
- selection methods.

In practice

You need to be careful. Although employers accept that they can no longer advertise for 'Girl Fridays', the Act makes a number of common job titles questionable, or even unlawful. For example:

- **manageress** implies that the vacancy is for a woman (although the term 'manager' is acceptable as it is commonly used regardless of gender)
- **policeman** is now police officer
- **matron** is now nurse manager
- **headmaster/mistress** is now headteacher
- **salesman** is now salesperson.

Further help

This is a detailed Act that affects every aspect of the recruitment process. Fortunately there is plenty of help to hand. The Equal

Opportunities Commission publishes a Code of Practice on Sex Discrimination, which gives guidance to employers and employment agencies on measures that can be taken to achieve equality between men and women. Further details are available from their website: www.eoc.org.uk

In addition, they have an excellent guide to advertisement wording and illustration, featuring examples of actual recruitment advertisements that come close to breaking the law.

Race Relations Act 1976/Race Relations Amendment Act 2000

The Race Relations Act 1976 and the Race Relations Amendment Act 2000 make it unlawful to discriminate on the grounds of race. Race can be defined in terms of:

- racial group
- colour
- nationality
- ethnic origin.

The Act applies to Great Britain only (England, Scotland and Wales). There is a separate Race Relations Order that applies to Northern Ireland. The Act covers all employers regardless of their size, and provides protection to all employees including vocational trainees and agency workers.

All aspects of the employment relationship are covered including:

- recruitment and selection
- promotion
- transfer
- training and development
- pay and benefits
- redundancy
- dismissal
- terms and conditions.

The Act includes provision for direct and indirect discrimination, as well as victimization. You can find practical, up-to-date information about the Act from the Commission for Racial Equality. Their website is www.cre.gov.uk.

The Race Relations Amendment Act 2000 came into force on 2 April 2001. It requires public authorities to have due regard to:

- eliminate racial discrimination
- promote equality of opportunity and good relations between people of different racial groups.

With regard to recruitment procedures, public bodies should monitor the recruitment, selection and progression of ethnic minority staff (and students) by grade, type of contract, pay and other benefits.

Exceptions

There are a limited number of exceptions to the above legislation. These are when being of a particular sex or race can be regarded as a genuine occupational qualification (GOQ). Examples include:

- actors or dramatists playing a specific role
- overseas workers, where the laws of the country worked in prohibit certain races, or gender, from doing the work.

Further details of these exceptions are available from the Campaign for Racial Equality website at www.cre.gov.uk.

Disability Discrimination Act 1995

The Disability Discrimination Act 1995 introduced new measures designed to end the discrimination which many people with disabilities face.

It protects such people in areas of:

- employment
- access to goods, facilities and services
- the management, buying or renting of land or property
- education.

Many of the Act's measures became law for employers in December 1996. Others are being phased in gradually.

With regard to recruitment and employment:

- It is unlawful to treat people with disabilities less favourably than other people for a reason related to their disability.
- Employers must make reasonable adjustments for people with disabilities, such as providing extra help or amending the job role.
- From 2004, employers may have to make reasonable adjust-

ments to the physical features of their premises to overcome physical barriers to access. Obvious examples include ramps, lifts and other means to ease access.

Further information is available from the Disability Rights Commission. They publish an excellent Code of Practice, copies of which can be ordered by telephone, or downloaded from their website: www.drc-gb.org.

taking it further

Some useful websites

www.personneltoday.com
The website for HR professionals

www.ipd.co.uk
Chartered Institute of Personnel and Development

www.businesslink.org
The National Business Advice Service

www.statistics.gov.uk
National Statistics Online, including national employment and training statistics

www.monster.co.uk
Currently one of the leading online recruitment websites

www.fish4jobs.co.uk
Currently one of the leading online recruitment websites

www.workthing.com
Currently one of the leading online recruitment websites

www.eoc.org.uk
Equal Opportunities Commission

www.equalitydirect.org.uk
Equality Direct

www.cre.gov.uk
Commission for Racial Equality

www.drc-gb.org
Disability Rights Commission

Books

Recruitment and Selection: A Competency Approach (Developing Practice)
Gareth Roberts, 1997, Chartered Institute of Personnel and Development

A Manager's Guide to Recruitment & Selection
Margaret Dale, 2003, Kogan Page

Competency-based Recruitment and Selection: A Practical Guide (Strategic Human Resource Management)
Robert Wood and Tim Payne, John Wiley and Sons Ltd

Employee Recruitment and Retention Handbook
Diane Arthur, 2001, Amacom

Recruitment and Selection (Professional Manager)
Financial Times, 1999, Prentice Hall

UK Recruitment Guide 2001
Philip Rawlinson and Zoe Foster, McGraw-Hill Education – Europe

Successful Graduate Recruitment
Jean Brading, 1998, Hawksmere Ltd

Readymade Job Advertisements: A Recruitment Toolkit for Every Manager
Neil Wenborn, 1991, Kogan Page

Principles and Practices of Recruitment Advertising
Bernard S. Hodes, 1982, Frederick Fell Publishers

The Difficult Hire: Seven Recruitment and Selection Principles for Hard to Fill Positions (Career Savvy Series)
Dennis Doverspike and Rhonda C. Tuel, 2000, Impact Publications

index